EAMONT BRIDGE, MAYBURGH HENGE 1893   32935P

ANCIENT BRITAIN

LAND OF MYSTERY AND LEGEND

WITH PHOTOGRAPHS FROM THE FRANCIS FRITH COLLECTION

COMPILED AND EDITED BY

ELIZA SACKETT AND JULIA SKINNER

THE FRANCIS FRITH COLLECTION

First published in the United Kingdom in 2006 by The Francis Frith Collection

Hardback edition ISBN 10: 1-84589-276-3
ISBN 13: 978-1-8458-9276-0

British Library Cataloguing in Publication Data

Ancient Britain
Compiled and edited by Eliza Sackett and Julia Skinner

The Francis Frith Collection
Frith's Barn, Teffont,
Salisbury, Wiltshire SP3 5QP
Tel: +44 (0) 1722 716 376
Email: info@francisfrith.co.uk
www.francisfrith.com

Designed and assembled by Terence Sackett

Printed in Singapore by Imago

Front Cover: Stonehenge 1887 *19797t*

CONTENTS

FRANCIS FRITH
VICTORIAN PIONEER

FRANCIS FRITH, founder of the world-famous photographic archive, was a complex and multi-talented man. A devout Quaker and a highly successful Victorian businessman, he was philosophical by nature and pioneering in outlook.

By 1855 he had already established a wholesale grocery business in Liverpool, and sold it for the astonishing sum of £200,000, which is the equivalent today of over £15,000,000. Now a very rich man, he was able to indulge his passion for travel. As a child he had pored over travel books written by early explorers, and his fancy and imagination had been stirred by family holidays to the sublime mountain regions of Wales and Scotland. 'What lands of spirit-stirring and enriching scenes and places!' he had written. He was to return to these scenes of grandeur in later years to 'recapture the thousands of vivid and tender memories', but with a different purpose. Now in his thirties, and captivated by the new science of photography, Frith set out on a series of pioneering journeys up the Nile and to the Near East that occupied him from 1856 until 1860.

INTRIGUE AND EXPLORATION

These far-flung journeys were packed with intrigue and adventure. In his life story, written when he was sixty-three, Frith tells of being held captive by bandits, and of fighting 'an awful midnight battle to the very point of surrender with a deadly pack of hungry, wild dogs'. Wearing flowing Arab costume, Frith arrived at Akaba by camel sixty years before Lawrence of Arabia, where he encountered 'desert princes and rival sheikhs, blazing with jewel-hilted swords'.

He was the first photographer to venture beyond the sixth cataract of the Nile. Africa was still the mysterious 'Dark Continent', and Stanley and Livingstone's historic meeting was a decade into the future. The conditions for picture taking confound belief. He laboured for hours in his wicker dark-room in the sweltering heat of the desert, while the volatile chemicals fizzed dangerously in their trays. Back in London he exhibited his photographs and was 'rapturously cheered' by members of the Royal Society. His reputation as a photographer was made overnight.

VENTURE OF A LIFE-TIME

Characteristically, Frith quickly spotted the opportunity to create a new business as a specialist publisher of photographs. He lived in an era of immense and sometimes violent change. For the poor in the early part of Victoria's reign work was exhausting and the hours long, and people had precious little free time to enjoy themselves. Most had no transport other than a cart or gig at their disposal, and rarely travelled far beyond the boundaries of their own town or village. However, by the 1870s the railways had threaded their way across the country, and Bank Holidays and half-day Saturdays had been made obligatory by Act of Parliament. All of a sudden the working man and his family were able to enjoy days out and see a little more of the world.

With typical business acumen, Francis Frith foresaw that these new tourists would enjoy having souvenirs to commemorate their days out. In 1860 he married Mary Ann Rosling and set out on a new career: his aim was to photograph every city, town and village in Britain. For the next thirty years he travelled the country by train and by pony and trap, producing fine photographs of seaside resorts and beauty spots that were keenly bought by millions of Victorians. These prints were painstakingly pasted into family albums and pored over during the dark nights of winter, rekindling memories of summer excursions.

THE RISE OF FRITH & CO

Frith's studio was soon supplying retail shops all over the country. To meet the demand he gathered about him a small team of photographers, and published the work of independent artist-photographers of the calibre of Roger Fenton and Francis Bedford. In order to gain some understanding of the scale of Frith's business one only has to look at the catalogue issued by Frith & Co in 1886: it runs to some 670 pages, listing not only many thousands of views of the British Isles but also many photographs of most European countries, and China, Japan, the USA and Canada. By 1890 Frith had created the greatest specialist photographic publishing company in the world, with over 2,000 sales outlets - more than the combined number that Boots and WH Smith have today!

POSTCARD BONANZA

The ever-popular holiday postcard we know today took many years to develop. The Post Office issued the first plain cards in 1870, with a pre-printed stamp on one face. In 1894 they allowed other publishers' cards to be sent through the mail with an attached adhesive halfpenny stamp. Demand grew rapidly, and in 1895 a new size of postcard was permitted called the court card, but there was little room for illustration. In 1899, a year after Frith's death, a new card measuring 5.5 x 3.5 inches became the standard format, but it was not until 1902 that the divided back came into being, so that the address and message

could be on one face and a full-size illustration on the other. Frith & Co were in the vanguard of postcard development: Frith's sons Eustace and Cyril continued their father's monumental task, expanding the number of views offered to the public and recording more and more places in Britain.

Francis Frith had died in 1898 at his villa in Cannes, his great project still growing. The archive he created continued in business for another seventy years. By 1970 it contained over a third of a million pictures showing 7,000 British towns and villages.

FRANCIS FRITH'S LEGACY

Frith's legacy to us today is of immense significance and value, for the magnificent archive of evocative photographs he created provides a unique record of change in the cities, towns and villages throughout Britain over a century and more. Frith and his fellow studio photographers revisited locations many times down the years to update their views, compiling for us an enthralling and colourful pageant of British life and character.

We are fortunate that Frith was dedicated to recording the minutiae of everyday life, for it is this sheer wealth of visual data, the painstaking chronicle of changes in dress, transport, street layouts, buildings, housing and landscape that captivates us so much today. His images offer us a powerful link with the past and with the lives of our ancestors.

THE VALUE OF THE ARCHIVE TODAY

Historians consider The Francis Frith Collection to be of prime national importance. It is the only archive of its kind remaining in private ownership. The archive's future is both bright and exciting. Francis Frith, with his unshakeable belief in making photographs available to the greatest number of people, would undoubtedly approve of the computer technology that allows his work to be rapidly transmitted to people all over by way of the internet. His photographs depicting our shared past are now bringing pleasure and enlightenment to millions around the world a century and more after his death.

INTRODUCTION

Up until the mid 19th century the study of ancient monuments was left to antiquarians, in the main amateur enthusiasts who pursued their studies independently of each other. There was no organised scientific discipline, for archaeology was not considered a subject worthy of proper study. It is not surprising that many of them did little to dispel the superstition and ignorance that surrounded antiquities and their origins, and even antiquarians of the calibre of William Stukeley were attributing anything they could not explain to the Druids. There was also much unfortunate dabbling by farmers and landowners in the early 19th century: they would recruit two or three labourers – all delighted to be away from the drudgery of field work – to hack away at a barrow or cromlech in the hope of finding gold and other valuables. No records or measurements were generally kept, and many important monuments were lost and destroyed as a consequence.

It was not until later in the Victorian era that archaeology came of age, and men of the calibre of Pitt Rivers and Colt Hoare began to alter attitudes. They encouraged an academic engagement with the past, shifting the emphasis of antiquarianism towards a more scientific study of ancient civilizations. By way of processes of rigorous measurement, accurate recording and drawing, the use of models and the dissemination of results in papers, books and journals, they turned archaeology into a serious and respectable academic discipline. Unlike their predecessors, they were happy turning up nothing more spectacular than a couple of skulls, a cracked sepulchre urn and some sherds of pottery – seemingly insignificant but full of import to the specialist. Folklore and legend were not entirely discarded or discredited, however, for they often offered important clues to the true functions and origins of individual momuments or remains.

Antiquarian societies sprung up during the second half of the Victorian period, and archaeology grew in popularity by leaps and bounds. The very fact that the Frith photographers recorded so many of our antiquities is proof of a new and widespread interest – it could not have been easy hauling heavy brass cameras and tripods into often inaccessible country.

The Frith photographs are of particular interest for us today, for they show many monuments before modern-day restoration. The earlier images are hugely atmospheric, some of the monuments having been recorded in often bleak and bare settings, without a turnstile or ticket-collector in sight. They offer us a fascinating insight into how our predecessors perceived antiquities and the ancient world.

KING ARTHUR'S CASTLE

Tintagel, Cornwall

This atmospheric site is on the north coast of Cornwall, overlooking the sea, and was described by Geoffrey of Monmouth in the 1100s as the birthplace of King Arthur. Geoffrey's description of the area is so accurate that it is believed that he visited the site himself: 'The castle is built high above the sea, which surrounds it on all sides, and there is no other way in except that offered by a narrow isthmus of rock'. The name 'Tintagel' derives from the Old Cornish 'din' or 'tin' (fortress) and 'tagel' (constriction or narrows). There have been several archaeological excavations here, which have uncovered the remains of dozens of huts from the 5th century AD. It appears that the area was an important centre of trade, with Cornish tin being exchanged for oil, wine, and other luxury goods from the Mediterranean; the prosperity of the area can be judged from the fact that more sherds of imported pottery have been found at Tintagel that at all the other sites of similar period in Britain and Ireland combined.

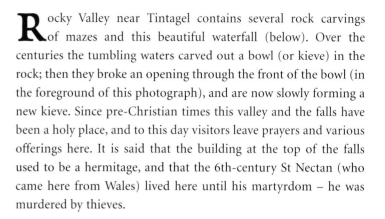

MERLIN

Left: TINTAGEL,
KING ARTHUR'S CASTLE AND
MERLIN'S CAVE C1960 T52208

Right: TINTAGEL,
ST NECTAN'S KIEVE FALLS 1894
33626A

Rocky Valley near Tintagel contains several rock carvings of mazes and this beautiful waterfall (below). Over the centuries the tumbling waters carved out a bowl (or kieve) in the rock; then they broke an opening through the front of the bowl (in the foreground of this photograph), and are now slowly forming a new kieve. Since pre-Christian times this valley and the falls have been a holy place, and to this day visitors leave prayers and various offerings here. It is said that the building at the top of the falls used to be a hermitage, and that the 6th-century St Nectan (who came here from Wales) lived here until his martyrdom – he was murdered by thieves.

The Arthur Stone discovered?

During an excavation in 1998 a piece of rock was uncovered bearing a Runic inscription dating from the 500s, which includes the name 'Artognov', or 'Arthnou'. This caused great excitement in the media and was promptly dubbed 'the Arthur Stone', and was hailed as proof of the Arthurian connection with Tintagel. However, Dr Geoffrey Wainwright, chief archaeologist with English Heritage, said: 'Despite the obvious temptation to link the Arthnou stone to either the historical or the legendary figure of Arthur, it must be stressed there is no evidence to make this connection. Nevertheless it proves for the first time that the name existed at that time and that the stone belonged to a person of status.'

KING ARTHUR

It is believed that King Arthur may have been a real person, but beyond that there is little agreement about who he was, what he did or even when he lived. None of the early sources refer to him as a king. He appears to have been a British leader who opposed the Saxon invasions. It seems that every historic town in Britain with strong Celtic connections claims a stake in the life of Arthur. Where romance ends and myth begins seems unimportant, so ingrained has he become in our historic culture. He is traditionally associated with the victory at Mount Badon around the year AD520. The story of Arthur, his knights of the Round Table and the return of his sword Excalibur to the Lady of the Lake is an exciting fable. That it cannot be accurately verified hardly seems to matter. Many places make a claim to be either the burial place of King Arthur or the site of his last battle, in the earliest accounts said to be Camlann, whose name means crooked bank, or glen.

KING ARTHUR'S GRAVE

Camelford, Cornwall

Top: CAMELFORD, KING ARTHUR'S GRAVE 1906   56167

Above: CAMELFORD, THE GRAVE OF KING ARTHUR C1960
C15009

Opposite: CAMELFORD, ROUGH TOR 1894   33593

It was Geoffrey of Monmouth, more a storyteller than a historian (he published his 'History of the Kings of Britain' in about 1136), who promulgated the legend of Arthur and his wizard Merlin, which was extended and colourfully embroidered in the medieval period. At least one of Geoffrey's contemporaries took the legends seriously: 'This is that Arthur of whom the trifling of the Britons talks such nonsense even today; a man clearly worthy not to be dreamed of in fallacious fables, but to be proclaimed in veracious histories.' (William of Malmesbury, 'Deeds of the Kings of the English', first published in 1125).

Geoffrey of Monmouth

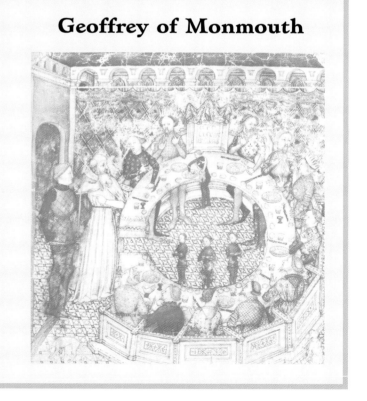

ROUGH TOR

Camelford, Cornwall

The second highest part of Bodmin Moor is Rough Tor, at 1,311ft (33593, above). The Tor has two granite outcrops which nature has evolved to form stacks of impressive bun-like stones; otherwise the moor is bleak and treeless. This outcrop is inside a stone fort, where the remains of hut circles belonging to the Neolithic period or early Bronze Age have been found.

HARLYN BAY

Padstow, Cornwall

These Victorian or Edwardian ladies are looking at the Iron Age cemetery that was discovered here in 1900. A major find, with 130 graves, the dig was supervised by a Mr Reddie-Mallet, and one of the diggers was the Rev Sabine Baring-Gould, author of 'Onward Christian Soldiers'.

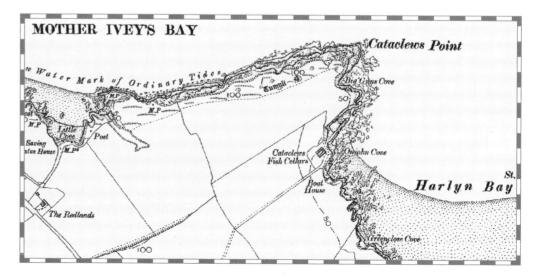

Above: HARLYN BAY, EXCAVATIONS 1901 47728
Right: HARLYN BAY, EXCAVATIONS 1901 47727

CRANTOCK

The Church

Carantoc and the dove

The village of Crantock is named after the 6th-century St Carantoc. He sailed here from Ireland, bringing a dove with him, which flew inland with a twig in its beak; where the dove dropped the twig, Carantoc decided to build his small oratory.

The foundations of Crantock's parish church, dedicated to St Carantoc, are pre-Norman, but the earliest features that we can see today date from Norman times – these are the choir arcades, just visible in the background of 33532 (page 13), and the font (in the foreground). The church became a collegiate church in the 13th century, but the college was closed down at the Dissolution of the Monasteries under Henry VIII. The church was enlarged and altered over the centuries, and restored at the end of the 19th century (by Sedding); photograph 33532 was taken before the restoration, and before the insertion of the rood screen in 1905, which was carved by Mary Rashleigh Pinwell, a vicar's daughter from Devon. The fine stained-glass windows (64827, left) tell the story of St Carantoc. In the churchyard is an interesting stone coffin (33533, above), which may be prehistoric.

TREVORNICK HOLY WELL

Holywell Bay, Cornwall

Top: HOLYWELL BAY, TREVORNICK HOLY WELL 1937 88238

Above: HOLYWELL BAY, TREVORNICK HOLY WELL 1937 88238A

Right: HOLYWELL BAY, TREVORNICK HOLY WELL 1937 88239

The lack of a church near this holy well suggests that it has been a sacred site since pre-Christian times. The well house is medieval. The water springs from a rock into a basin, and then flows down to the sea.

THE LOST CHURCH AND THE CROSS

Perranporth, Cornwall

Perrans Bay is traditionally the landing place of St Piran, who, legend tells us, sailed across the sea on a granite millstone in the 5th century. He later became the patron saint of Cornish tinners. The ruin of an early Christian oratory was discovered buried in the dunes of Penhale Sands in the 19th century. Because of its early date and its association with St Piran it was given protection from the elements and blown sands by the building of a rather unattractive shell (see 66666), but this was all deliberately reburied again in 1981. Also within the dunes close by the oratory is this ancient cross, known as St Piran's Cross.

Above: PERRANPORTH, THE LOST CHURCH NEAR HOLYWELL 1914   66666

Right: PERRANPORTH, THE CROSS NEAR THE BURIED CHURCH 1893   31837

CARN BREA *Penzance, Cornwall*

Rock Bason Coit at Karnbre.

Above left: CARN BREA 1906 56457

Above right: CARN BREA, THE MONUMENT 1891 29855

This hill near Redruth has seen human activity over a long stretch of time. Surrounding the monument (a granite obelisk 30m high erected in 1836 to Sir Francis Basset, Lord de Dunstanville, a local mine owner) and the ruins of a medieval castle are the famous Carn Brea remains. This is possibly the oldest known Neolithic settlement in England; it dates from about 3,000 to 3,500BC. Near the medieval castle (to the left in 56457, above) is an enclosure defined by a ruinous stone wall and a ditch, where huts and rock shelters have been found; it has been calculated that this would have taken about 30,000 hours to construct. This enclosure lies within extensive ramparts, implying that this was a defensive site. Indeed, about a third of the flint and stone artefacts found here were arrowheads. A hoard of Bronze Age axes has also been found here.

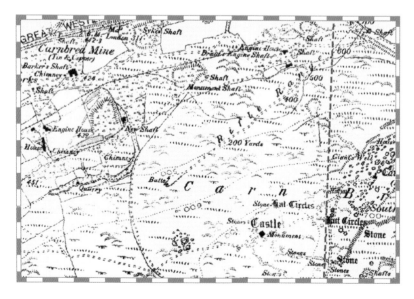

Merry dancers turned into stone

Legend has it that the stones are maidens and pipers who were turned into stone for dancing on the Sabbath Day – two standing stones north of the circle (but not visible from it) are called the Pipers, and one plainly visible to the west (the Goon Rith standing stone) is known as the Fiddler. The circle itself is also known as the Dawn's Men, a corruption of 'Dans Maen', 'stone dance'.

Situated near St Buryan, the Merry Maidens stone circle is one of the most complete stone circles in Cornwall, and consists of nineteen stones. The granite pillars are evenly spaced in a circle about 24m in diameter, and are graded in height, the tallest to the south-south-west. It is an exact circle, but it appears to have no astronomical significance. It is interesting that the nearby circle of Boscawen-un also has nineteen stones. This view shows the entrance to the circle on the far side, just to the left.

Above: PENZANCE, THE MERRY MAIDENS C1864 2030

Near the Madron-Morvah road in west Cornwall, this Neolithic burial chamber was restored in 1824 after the capstone had fallen to the ground during a storm in 1815. It stands today about 1.5m high, but it was most certainly originally higher – 18th-century records report that 'it was so high that a man could sit on horseback beneath it'. At the time of its construction, this stone chamber might have had a long cairn around it; the chamber was originally at the northern end of the cairn. Local legend says that King Arthur used the stone top as a dining table just before his last battle.

LANYON QUOIT	*Penzance, Cornwall*

Lanyon Gromleh Cornwall.

PENZANCE, LANYON QUOIT 1890   22985P

Barrows, the burial places of the ancients

Long Barrows

Long barrows, or chambered tombs, were the established burial practice during the Neolithic period (c3,700-2,500BC). The Neolithic people in the West Country usually built tombs with a single chamber; elsewhere in the country the tombs could contain five or more separate compartments. Geography and the ease of readily-available building materials probably played a part in determining custom and practice. The custom seems to have been to allow the body to decompose; then, probably after a ritualistic ceremony, the bones would often be rearranged within a chamber, often together with the bones of others. Over the chamber or chambers a massive earthen mound or cairn was piled, which could be clearly seen and recognised as a special resting place for the bones of the dead.

Round Barrows

Burials in the Bronze Age tended to differ, depending on whether burials belonged to the Early Bronze Age or the later Middle and Late Bronze Age. Early Bronze Age peoples mostly buried contracted skeletons, possibly to signify the re-birth or sleeping position, and the burial was generally accompanied by a beaker of hand-made pottery.

In the case of the most famous barrow, Bush Barrow, near Stonehenge, the skeleton of a man lying from south to north was found in 1808. At his side were two Bronze Age daggers, one with a wooden hilt decorated with thousands of minute gold pins.

Near his leg was a mace, symbol of a chieftain perhaps, an axe and the remains of a wooden shield decorated with bronze. A lozenge-shaped gold plate was at his chest, and an engraved hook of hammered gold at his waist. This has been by far the most glamorous discovery of a Bronze Age tomb; it reveals how far man had progressed since the days of the early Neolithic people. The Middle and Later Bronze Age people tended to cremate their dead and put the remains in an urn, which was often inverted and placed at the bottom of the barrow before being covered with the traditional earthen mound.

PENZANCE CROSSES

Penzance, Cornwall

In the churchyard of St Mary's at Penzance is this remnant of a granite cross, depicting the Virgin and Child. It is believed that this originally came from a headland chapel dedicated to St Gabriel and St Raphael which was sited near the harbour; the name Penzance comes from 'Pen Sans', 'holy headland'. Headland chapels are a feature of Cornwall. They were not only shrines to saints known to protect travellers, but were also used as navigational aids and lookout posts.

In Victorian times many old Celtic crosses and other monuments were 'recycled' as the designs became fashionable. This one was moved to the Victorian Morrab Gardens near the seafront in Penzance.

Above: PENZANCE, ST MARY'S CHURCHYARD, A CROSS FRAGMENT 1908 59466

Right: PENZANCE, AN OLD CROSS IN MORRAB GARDENS 1906 56518

St Buryan, near Penzance, is now thought to have been an important Celtic monastic site. The churchyard contains several strange, small carved crossheads (this is a typical example), along with a crucifix figure dating from the 10th century.

ST BURYÁN CROSSES | *Penzance, Cornwall*

Above: ST BURYAN, A CROSS 1903 50859

Right: ST BURYAN, A CROSS 1890 27745

en an Tol means 'stone of the hole'; this most famous of Cornish landmarks may belong to the Neolithic period or Bronze Age. Since this photograph was taken, the site has been tidied and the ground worn smooth by visitors. Has some of this ancient monument disappeared through time? Are the three stones in their original positions? Were they once part of a stone row or a Bronze Age stone circle? It seems most likely that they were originally part of the chamber of a Neolithic long barrow, and the holed stone was the portal through which the dead were carried, inwards for burial, outwards as bones to be used in sacred rites.

Through the hole and back to health

Inevitably, legends and myths concerning the use of Men an Tol abound: it is said that children were passed through the hole to cure rickets and skin diseases. Adults who were sufficiently slim could ward off fevers by crawling through the hole nine times 'widdershins' (anti-clockwise, or anti-sunwise).

THE MEN SCRYFÁ

Madron, Cornwall

ear the village of Madron, to the north of Penzance, is the 8ft-tall Men Scryfa, which means 'written stone'. On it is a vertical inscription, 'Rialobranus Cunovali filius', 'Rialobran son of Cunoval', which dates from the 6th century – the stone itself may be a prehistoric standing stone. It is an impressive yet sad monument standing lonely on the bare moor; its meaning is a mystery. Legend says that this is the grave of a king killed in battle – he was as tall as his gravestone.

Opposite: MADRON, MEN AN TOL 1890 22986P

Above: MADRON, THE MEN SCRYFÁ 1890 22987

The Archangel himself appears in this 'chair' when a storm is raging

'St Michael's Mount, that extraordinary combination, geologically speaking, of granite and clay-slate … is as interesting a place to visit as it is beautiful to look upon. The views from its summit over sea and land are of surpassing loveliness, and to enjoy them to the full it is not necessary to make the hazardous attempt to sit in 'St Michael's Chair', the half, it is said, of an old stone lantern, overhanging the precipice in a very perilous way. The villagers around the bay will tell you that the archangel himself appears in this 'chair' when a storm is raging, and firmly believe that he is the guardian spirit of the seas.'

THE REV SAMUEL MANNING 1885

St Michael's Mount, a tiny island off Marazion not far from Land's End, was a port and a trading centre for tin and copper from as early as 350BC. However, after the Roman invasion in the 1st century, it became a holy place frequented by hermits and saints. St Keyne is supposed to have visited in the late 5th century – a spring miraculously gushed forth when she stepped on to the island. Legend says that St Keyne also gave a stone seat the power to grant the upper hand in marriage, depending on who managed to sit on it first. The island became a popular place of pilgrimage after a fisherman saw a vision of St Michael: according to different versions of the legend, the saint appeared either high upon a rocky ledge, or walking upon the waters of Mounts Bay. St Michael's Mount went on to attract pilgrims from all over the country for the next 1,500 years. Over that time a church and priory has been built on the island, and also a fortified castle, later the home of the St Aubyn family. Today St Michael's Mount is managed by the National Trust – as well as tourists, religious pilgrims still visit here. There are four ancient crosses on St Michael's Mount in Cornwall – an example is the one we see in 60999 (opposite, centre). All the crosses shown opposite have been brought here from elsewhere.

THE ISLES OF SCILLY

THE ISLES OF SCILLY, ST MARY'S, OLD TOWN 1891 28457

The Isles of Scilly are a small group of islands lying some 30 miles to the west of Land's End. They form a ring enclosing a stretch of calmer sea, which provides a refuge from the rough Atlantic. The islands appear to have been occupied, on and off, since the Stone Age. On a clear day they can be seen from Land's End, and it was only a question of whose boat was best, or who had luck with the weather, for the first settlers to step ashore, marvelling at the calm of the inner shores of the islands, with their abundance of birds and shellfish on the rocks. The islands were bigger then, and some of them, notably Bryher, Samson and Tresco, were joined together in places.

Both the Phoenicians and the Romans knew of these islands, which were reputed to produce tin. Prehistoric peoples buried their dead on what were known formerly as the Isles of the Blessed, in the path of the setting sun. As the islands were remote and often hidden by clouds or mist, they were used by the Romans as a place of banishment, and in the Middle Ages they were the haunt of pirates and marauders. Hermits were also brave enough to live and pray in ancient caves and tombs on the islands. It is said that one of these hermits, St Elid, converted King Olaf of Norway to Christianity when he came to burn and pillage. St Elid's Isle is better known today as St Helen's, which contains the remains of a pest house, where sailors from plague-ridden ships were put in quarantine.

Totmen Northwethel Scilly.

The islanders threw pins into this well (S73007a, left) and prayed 'for a wreck before morning' and other benefits. The waters were believed to be healing. The islanders celebrated the feast of St Warna, which was on 13 January, with great gusto.

The biggest logan stone on St Agnes, the Giant's Punchbowl, was described by Dr Borlase in 1756 as easily rocked 'by being touched by a pole from below' (31155, above).

Left: THE ISLES OF SCILLY, ST AGNES, THE HOLY WELL OF ST WARNA C1955 S73007A

Above: THE ISLES OF SCILLY, ST AGNES, THE GIANT'S PUNCHBOWL 1892 31155

On the downs to the south near Camperdizel lies the well-known Troy Town Maze (S73004a, opposite left). It is thought by some to be very old, even of Phoenician origin. A lighthouse keeper, Amos Clarke, is supposed to have 'reworked' it in the early 18th century. A recent dowser found traces of a very ancient slightly different layout underneath the present-day pebbles. Strictly speaking, this should not be called a maze; in fact it is a labyrinth – the path leads straight to the centre and out again.

The Loaded Camel (31127, above) presents a quirky landmark. Unlike many of the rock formation names, this one seems to fit exactly.

Fabled Lyonesse

The Scilly Islands, just visible [from Cornwall] in clear weather on the far horizon, are held to be surviving relics of that drowned land of Lyonesse, so famous in Arthuric legend. But geologists insist that the disappearance of such a tract is, under the circumstances, an impossibility …
VICTORIAN GUIDEBOOK

Opposite: THE ISLES OF SCILLY, ST AGNES, THE ANCIENT PEBBLE MAZE C1955 S73004A
Above: THE ISLES OF SCILLY, ST MARY'S, THE LOADED CAMEL 1892 31127

ANCIENT CROSS · *Mylor, Cornwall*

MYLOR, THE ANCIENT CROSS C1960 M111004

The church at Mylor near Penzance is dedicated to the Celtic saint St Melorus, or St Mylor, who is believed to have established the first church in the area, and after whom the village is named. The ancient cross has now been re-erected in the churchyard, but local tradition says that it originally marked the site of the saint's grave.

FOUR TURNINGS CROSS

Fowey, Cornwall

Tristan and Iseult

The story of Tristan's love for Iseult is one of the world's great love stories: Tristan went to Ireland to escort Iseult back as King Mark's bride, but they drank the love potion intended for Iseult and Mark, and fell inescapably in love, with tragic consequences.

This inscribed stone, 7ft tall, stands at a crossroads near Fowey in this photograph. It was moved there from Castle Dore, a nearby Iron Age hill-fort, but has since been moved nearer the town. The inscription (the stone itself may have been erected earlier) is reputed to date from the 6th century. Though it is now too difficult to read, it was said to be: 'Drustanus hic iacet Cunomori filius', 'Here lies Drustanus, the son of Cunomorus'. Some believe that this refers to Sir Tristan, immortalised in several Arthurian romances, the nephew of King Mark of Cornwall, who was said to have lived at Castle Dore in the 6th century. Could it be that this stone refers to the Tristan of legend? In the mid 20th century, excavators at Castle Dore found what they believed was evidence for a complex of timber buildings dating from the 5th or 6th centuries, the possible site of King Mark's palace. However, further research in the 1980s failed in fact to find any evidence that Castle Dore was occupied after Iron Age times, and the earliest account of the Tristan and Iseult story is in a French poem of the 12th century.

ANCIENT CROSS AND WELL   *Polruan, Cornwall*

This is also known as the cross of St Saviour, whose ruined chapel is not far away (65964, left). The shaft of the cross is of Pentewan stone, but the fragment of cross head is granite, and perhaps from a different monument. The cross and the well next to it are situated near the top of the hill out of Polruan.

MENÁCUDDLE WELL

St Austell, Cornwall

The waters of this well were used to treat ulcers, and to bathe sick children. At one time the custom was to throw pins into the water to ensure good fortune, and it was believed that pins thrown by previous visitors would rise up from the bottom of the well to meet the new one. This custom has now been superseded by offering coins. The small well house was built in the 15th century, and restored in 1922.

Left: POLRUAN, THE ANCIENT CROSS AND THE WELL 1913 65964

Above: ST AUSTELL, MENACUDDLE WELL C1955 S6014

33

THE STONE CIRCLE

Duloe, Cornwall

South of Bodmin Moor stands this small, isolated Bronze Age stone circle, in fact a flattened circle in shape, measuring 11.9m by 11.3m metres in diameter. It has only eight stones, but these are noticeable for their size, up to 2.65m high. The stones, huge white unhewn blocks of quartz, may have been brought from the lead lode at Herodsfoot, about two miles away – it would have taken about 35 people to move the larger stones. They are aligned to the points of the compass, so it may be that astronomical observations were made here. However, the stones were re-erected in the 1860s, when the hedge that used to bisect the site was removed. In the process an urn dating from the mid 2nd millennium BC, and said to be full of bones, was discovered beside the largest stone, suggesting that funerary rituals were carried out here as well.

Cornwall's pilgrim route to Santiago

The ancient route crossing Cornwall from north to south is known today as the Saints' Way: Celtic Christians from Ireland and Wales would cross the Bristol Channel to Padstow, and then walk across Cornwall to Fowey. From Fowey they would go by sea to Spain and then follow the pilgrim route to Santiago.

Opposite:
DULOE, THE STONE
CIRCLE 1900   45909

Left:
LANLIVERY, THE ANCIENT CELTIC
CROSS 1903   49789

Right:
LOSTWITHIEL,
BOCONNOC, OLD CROSS 1898   41422A

The cross in 49789 (left) stands on the A390 road at a junction with the B3269 from Bodmin, which is seen in this photograph of over a century ago as a quiet lane. The Bodmin road follows an ancient ridgeway south towards Fowey, and the siting of the somewhat battered wayside cross would therefore seem to be significant. Crosses like the one in this photograph marked the pilgrim route known as the Saints' Way (see above).

ANCIENT CROSSES | *Lanlivery, Boconnoc, Cornwall*

THE HOLY WELL   *Roche, Cornwall*

The holy well at Roche was named after St Gundred, the daughter of a leper, who drew water for her father here; she is said to have lived in the chapel on top of Roche Rock. Lunatics were immersed in the water, but the water of the well was considered most efficacious by young unmarried girls, who would throw pins and needles into the water, and try to predict their fortune from the sparkling of the bubbles. The time for this custom was Holy Thursday (Maundy Thursday, the day before Good Friday), and the following two Thursdays, just before sunrise.

On Bodmin Moor stands the spectacular Neolithic burial chamber known as Trethevy Quoit – it is also known as the Trevethy Stones and the Giant's House (24475, right). John Norden, a Tudor visitor to Cornwall, described it as 'a little howse raysed of mightie stones, standing on a little hill within a fielde'. A rectangular chamber is formed by an H-shaped setting of upright stones, topped by a capstone. Here, six uprights (originally seven) form the walls, and the massive sloping capstone is 3.7m long. At its highest, the tomb stands 4.6m high. At some time an opening was cut in the front stone to allow access into the chamber, and there is a hole in the highest point of the capstone – it has been speculated that this might have some astronomical significance. The tomb was originally surrounded by a large oval mound; this was last recorded in the 19th century, but has now been almost obliterated by man and time.

THE TRETHEVY QUOIT

Liskeard, Cornwall

Liskeard, Cornwall

The granite stone of Bodmin Moor supports a natural oddity, the impressive outcrop known as the Cheesewring. The summit of the hill encloses a stone fort, probably associated with the Neolithic period or the Bronze Age.

You shrink from walking under it ...

The whole plain appeared like the site of an ancient city of palaces, overthrown and crumbled into atoms by an earthquake ... If a man dreamt of a great pile of stones in a nightmare, he would dream of such a pile as the Cheese-Wring ... When you first see it you instinctively shrink from walking under it. Beholding the tons on tons of stone balanced to a hair's breadth on the mere fragments beneath, you think that with a pole in your hand, with one push against the top rocks, you could hurl down the hill in an instant a pile which has stood for centuries, unshaken by the fiercest hurricane that ever blew, rushing from the great void of an ocean over the naked surface of the moor.

WILKIE COLLINS, 'RAMBLES BEYOND RAILWAYS' 1852

This was the home in the 18th century of a local stonecutter called Daniel Gumb, who tunnelled under the existing stones. All that is now left is a small part of his original home, which only had three rooms. In this cave-house Daniel brought up at least 9 children (he is thought to have had 13 children altogether, but some died young). On a stone beside the house is carved 'D GUMB 1735', which is said to be the date of Daniel's third marriage – potential wives were obviously not put off by the unusual living arrangements! Daniel Gumb died in 1773, and many of his children emigrated to America.

Opposite: LISKEARD, THE CHEESEWRING 1890 24476
Above left: LISKEARD, THE CHEESEWRING, LONG STONE C1960 L53004P
Above right: LISKEARD, THE CHEESEWRING, DANIEL GUMB'S HOUSE 1908 59773

THE HURLERS — *Liskeard, Cornwall*

The Hurlers, a highly important late Neolithic group of three stone circles, stand on Bodmin Moor amongst the remains of the later tin mining industry. Cheesewring Hill can be seen on the horizon. The circles are ranged in a line running NNE to SSW, and are all well over 30m in diameter. It is unusual that the granite stones were hammered into shape and are roughly of the same size; the chippings from the shaping were spread in the centre circle, and the northern circle was paved with granite. Why were there three circles here? In his 'The Stone Circles of the British Isles' (1976), Aubrey Burl tells us that multiple circles are relatively common in the south-west of Britain, and that they often stand, as the Hurlers do, where peoples and traders might well converge; perhaps the central (and largest) circle here was the first monument, and the others were added as the population grew and/or rituals became more complex.

Men transformed into stones

In his 'Britannia', first published in English in 1610, William Camden records a local legend: 'The neighbouring Inhabitants terme them Hurlers, as being by devout and godly error perswaded that they had been men sometime transformed into stones, for profaning the Lord's Day with hurling the ball'.

Long Tom (59769, above) is probably a Neolithic standing stone that has been Christianised by the carving of a cross on it. In the background it is just possible to see the chimney of an old copper mine.

LISKEARD, ST CLEER, DURNGARTH'S MONUMENT, OR THE KING STONE 1908 59770

The monument on the right of this photograph is known as King Doniert's Stone today. The short granite cross base with a carved interlace design is inscribed: 'Doniert rogavit pro anima', which translates as 'Doniert ordered this for the good of his soul'. It is thought that Doniert was Durngarth, King of Cornwall, who drowned in AD875, possibly in the River Fowey. The taller stone (7ft) is known as 'The Other Half Stone'; it also has intricate carving. It may be earlier in date and unrelated to the Doniert stone. Both shafts have rectangular sockets on the top which were probably for wooden crosses. The stones stand beside a lane to the north of St Cleer.

41

ST KEYNE'S WELL — *Liskeard, Cornwall*

Pilgrims have long sought the healing powers of sacred wells. It is thought that many wells were sacred in prehistoric and pre-Christian times, and early Christians would drink or even immerse themselves in holy water. Votive offerings were often thrown into the water; today, tourists often do the same by throwing coins into fountains and wells.

This is one of the most famous wells in Cornwall. St Keyne (born AD461) was a Welsh princess who refused to marry. She left her home and, after ridding Keynsham of serpents, she eventually arrived in Cornwall. She blessed this well with the power of conferring the upper hand in a marriage to whoever drank of it first, husband or wife.

The legend of St Keyne's Well was immortalised by the 19th-century poet Robert Southey:

A well there is in the west country,
And a clearer one never was seen;
There is not a wife in the west country
But has heard of the Well of St. Keyne.

An oak and an elm-tree stand beside,
And behind doth an ash-tree grow,
And a willow from the bank above
Droops to the water below.

A traveller came to the Well of St. Keyne;
Joyfully he drew nigh,
For from the cock-crow he had been travelling,
And there was not a cloud in the sky.

He drank of the water so cool and clear,
For thirsty and hot was he,
And he sat down upon the bank
Under the willow-tree.

There came a man from the house hard by
At the Well to fill his pail;
On the Well-side he rested it,
And he bade the stranger hail.

'Now art thou a bachelor, stranger?' quoth he,
'For an if thou hast a wife,
The happiest draught thou hast drank this day
That ever thou didst in thy life.

'Or has thy good woman, if one thou hast,
Ever here in Cornwall been?
For an if she have, I'll venture my life
She has drank of the Well of St. Keyne.'

'I have left a good woman who never was here.'
The stranger he made reply,
'But that my draught should be the better for that,
I pray you answer me why?'

'St. Keyne,' quoth the Cornish-man, 'many a time
Drank of this crystal well,
And before the Angel summon'd her,
She laid on the water a spell.

'If the husband of this gifted well
Shall drink before his wife,
A happy man thenceforth is he,
For he shall be master for life.

'But if the wife should drink of it first,—
God help the husband then!'
The stranger stoopt to the well of St. Keyne,
And drank of the water again.

'You drank of the Well I warrant betimes?'
He to the Cornish-man said:
But the Cornish-man smiled as the stranger spake,
And sheepishly shook his head.

'I hasten'd as soon as the wedding was done,
And left my wife in the porch;
But i' faith she had been wiser than me,
For she took a bottle to church.'

'THE WELL OF ST KEYNE'
ROBERT SOUTHEY (1774–1843)

Left: LISKEARD, ST KEYNE'S WELL 1906 56313P
Above: LISKEARD, ST KEYNE'S WELL 1938 88596

ST CLEER'S WELL *Liskeard, Cornwall*

On the edge of Bodmin Moor, near Liskeard, there are several important archaeological sites and Celtic crosses. Here we see St Cleer's holy well in the village named after him (88585, opposite). The well is protected by the charming 15th-century baptistery erected over it – the niche in the front gable holds a carving of a monk-like figure. The trickling waters of this well were said to have special powers to cure madness.

Opposite: ST CLEER, THE WELL 1938 88595

John Marius Wilson's 'Imperial Gazetteer of England and Wales' (1870–72) describes the well thus: 'St Cleer's well was anciently used as a ducking pool for insane persons; is enclosed by the ivy-clad ruin of a chapel; and adjoins an ancient cross, about 9 feet high'.

THE PIPE WELL

Liskeard, Cornwall

LISKEARD, THE PIPE WELL C1955 L53013

OLD CORNISH CROSS

Liskeard, Cornwall

Above: LISKEARD, AN OLD CORNISH CROSS 1928 81358

This wayside cross was brought to Liskeard church in 1908 after it was discovered being used as a gatepost on a nearby farm. Note the thin Latin cross incised on the shaft. The cross, which has been restored, is about 7ft high.

The Pipe Well is fed by four springs, and has never been known to run dry. The well was also known as the Well of St Martin. Its water was believed to have miraculous healing powers, and to be particularly good for eye disorders.

Some Cornish Holy Wells

DUPATH WELL

Callington

This well was probably a pre-Christian shrine. A local legend tells the tale of a Saxon maiden who was loved by two men: Gottlieb, a wealthy man and the preferred choice of the maiden's father, and the poor knight Sir Colan, who was the maiden's favourite. The two men fought over the maiden, and Gottlieb was slain. In remorse, Sir Colan built the well to atone for his deed, but he died of his own wounds soon after. Some folklorists have seen pagan origins to this tale, seeing it as a parallel for the duel between the lords of summer and winter over the goddess of spring. The water of this well was believed to cure whooping cough.

Left: CALLINGTON, DUPATH WELL 1890 24560

Opposite above left: LAUNCESTON, ST STEPHEN'S HOLY WELL 1911 63665

Opposite above right: ST NEOT, THE WELL 1893 32360

Opposite below left: BODMIN, ST GURON'S WELL 1938 88785

ST STEPHEN'S WELL *Launceston*

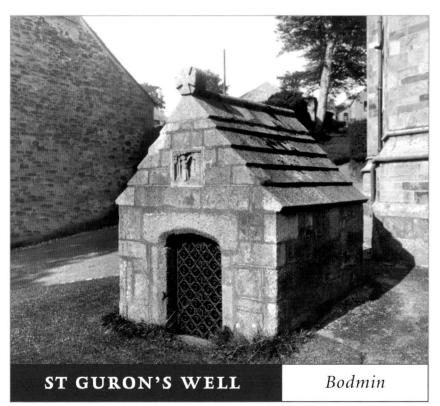

ST GURON'S WELL *Bodmin*

ST NEOT'S WELL *St Neot*

St Stephens, standing high on the north slope of the Kensey valley opposite Launceston, is an ancient settlement, pre-dating the town and possibly giving the origin of Launceston as a name – Lanstefan, in the old Cornish, translates as 'the church, or sacred enclosure, of Stephen'. The holy well dedicated to St Stephen (63665, above left), stands in a tranquil spot on Gallows Hill, overlooking the valley. The little building is probably not that old – 19th-century seems to be the local consensus.

The waters of St Neot's well were believed to cure sick children (32360, above right). The well also had a legend associated with it: St Neot used to stand in the water, reciting from the Psalter. One day he was shown three fish swimming in the well by an angel, and was told that each day he could take one fish to eat, but not to take more. During a period of illness St Neot sent his servant, Barius, to the well to collect his fish, but Barius caught and cooked two. St Neot ordered him to return both the cooked fish to the well, whereupon by a miracle they came back to life. This legend is commemorated in a stained glass window in St Neot's Church.

St Guron's Well (88785, left) is situated in the grounds of St Petroc's Church, Bodmin. It was thought that drinking the water of this well gave the power to foretell the future. Another ancient well near Bodmin is Scarlet's Well; at certain times of the year its water seems to show all the colours of the rainbow, which suggests that it runs through a mineral vein. The waters of this well were supposed to cure all kinds of diseases.

Some Cornish Crosses

CALLINGTON

ST COLUMB MAJOR

ST MAWGAN

Still standing outside Callington church is this very weathered lantern cross on a granite shaft (24559, 59729, opposite).

The cross shown in 59344 (below left) is now in the churchyard of St Mawgan-in-Pydar, and was brought here from its previous site in 1942.

The Quethioc Cross (59763) is a fine and typical example of a tall freestanding Cornish Celtic cross with a plain shaft and a wheel-headed cross.

Opposite left:
CALLINGTON, THE OLD CROSS
1890   24559

Opposite right:
CALLINGTON, THE OLD CROSS
1908   59729

Above left:
ST COLUMB MAJOR, A CROSS
IN THE CHURCHYARD
1901   47760

Below left:
ST MAWGAN, THE CROSS
1907   59344

Right: QUETHIOCK,
THE CELTIC CROSS 1908   59763

QUETHIOCK

BOWERMAN'S NOSE *Chagford, Devon*

SPINSTER'S ROCK

Chagford, Devon

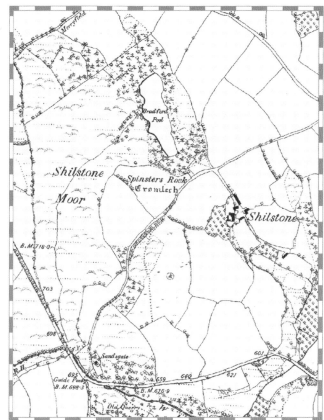

Far left: CHAGFORD, BOWERMAN'S NOSE C1871 5793

Near left: CHAGFORD, SPINSTER'S ROCK C1871 5801P

Above right: CHAGFORD, THE WEEK DOWN CROSS 1907 58484

The legend attached to the natural rock formation on Dartmoor of Bowerman's Nose (5793, far left) is that it is Bowerman the Hunter and his hounds, turned to stone by a coven of witches whom he disturbed whilst out hunting.

Spinster's Rock is in Devon, near Drewsteignton (5801p, near left). The three uprights are so-called because three spinsters are supposed to have erected the monument before breakfast! The covering earthen mound of what is actually a Neolithic chambered tomb has long since disappeared.

The Week Down cross (58484, above right) stands on the route between North Bovey and Chagford, and was probably erected to mark an ancient trackway. The cross was moved slightly back from its original position in 1867, but great care was taken to keep the exact angle of its lean. Both faces of the cross are inscribed with a Maltese cross; it is interesting that the cross on the eastern face is parallel with the main cross, whilst the cross on the western face is vertical to the ground.

CHAGFORD, A MOORLAND PATH BY A STONE CIRCLE 1924 76492

In Victorian times there was a fierce debate about the origins and dates of Dartmoor's stone circles and monuments. The antiquarian and photographer Robert Burnard writes with typical academic good sense in his 'Dartmoor Pictorial Records' of 1890:

If, as some writers contend, these erections date from within the Christian era, how is it that all tradition in connection with them has disappeared? And if the rude monoliths or menhirs on Dartmoor have been erected, we will say, not much more than a thousand years, how is it that, unlike the smaller menhirs or inscribed stones, which we know are fifth or sixth century work, they are all devoid of any indication of lettering? Surely the balance of evidence is in favour of remote antiquity for such objects as menhirs and the 'sacred' circles.

SCORHILL STONE CIRCLE *Chagford, Devon*

Negotiating Dartmoor has always been a precarious exercise in avoiding unmarked bogs, dense ferns and clay workings. Hence circles and standing stones also served as waymarkers, and sometimes as boundary markers (76492, opposite).

In the north-east corner of Dartmoor, in open country, is one of the finest stone rings, Scorhill (76494, left). It once consisted of 36 stones erected without any shaping. The circle dates from the Bronze Age. In the background of the photograph is the great boss of Kestor.

Rising to 1,433ft, the boss of Kestor serves as a prominent landmark with its outlying granite rocky basin, as seen when approaching from Chagford (76490, below). The slopes around Kestor Rocks are particularly rich in prehistoric archaeology, with evidence of both Neolithic and Bronze Age occupation, including the remains of a settlement with about 27 hut circles. Also to be seen are the associated field systems and boundary walls of the settlement, much of which was made from massive slabs of stone, set end-on into the ground.

Above: CHAGFORD, SCORHILL, A SACRED CIRCLE SHOWING KESTOR 1924 76494

Right: CHAGFORD, KESTOR ROCKS 1924 76490

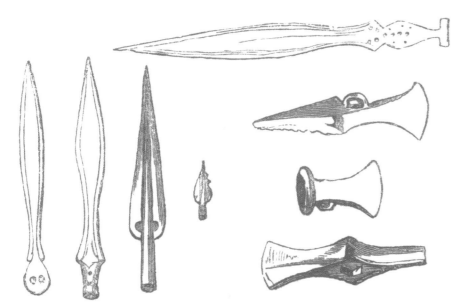

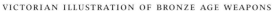

VICTORIAN ILLUSTRATION OF BRONZE AGE WEAPONS

KESTOR ROCKS *Chagford, Devon*

MARY JAY'S GRAVE

Chagford, Devon

Pregnant, abandoned – a tragic suicide

The grave at this lonely spot is believed to be the final resting place of Mary, or Kitty, Jay, a poor local girl who hung herself in a nearby barn after finding she was pregnant and was abandoned by the father, the local farmer's son. As suicides were not permitted burial in consecrated ground, the custom was for them to be interred at a crossroads, as in this case. Stories soon began to be told of a dark figure being seen kneeling beside the grave on moonlit nights, which some say is the ghost of the farmer's son, whose punishment was to watch over the grave of his tragic sweetheart and unborn child. The grave often has flowers and other offerings placed upon it, a tradition which began soon after the burial of Mary Jay, and which still continues to this day.

THE TOLMEN

River Teign, Devon

The name 'Tolmen' comes from the Celtic words 'tol' (hole) and 'maen' (stone), which accurately describes this large boulder lying on the bank of the Teign. The large hole goes right through the rock, and was formed by erosion. The hole is large enough for an adult to pass through; it was believed at one time that anyone doing so would be free from rheumatic disorders for life.

Above: CHAGFORD, MARY (KITTY) JAY'S GRAVE C1960 C559042

Right: DARTMOOR, THE TOLMEN STONE ON THE TEIGN C1871 5786

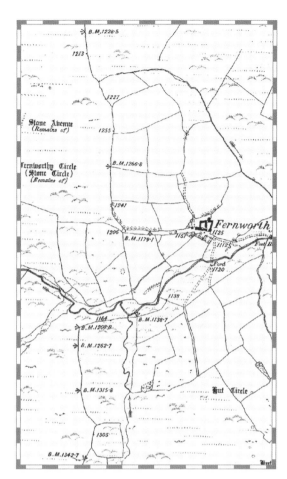

THE SACRED CIRCLE · *Fernworthy, Devon*

Fernworthy stone circle looks very different today, for it is surrounded by trees, and therefore nearer in appearance to the way it looked when it was constructed in the late Neolithic era. At that time, Dartmoor was not a treeless waste, but a wooded landscape dotted with clearings made by the early settlers. It is probable, given the number of stone circles found on Dartmoor, that each was erected by a family or group of families for ritual worship, either to venerate the dead or for an astronomical purpose. The entire inner area of Fernworthy circle was found to have been strewn with charcoal, implying that fire may have played a part in the rituals carried out here. The circle (in fact slightly flattened in shape) is about 20m in diameter, and is formed by 27 blocks of granite; these are graduated in height, which is most unusual for southern England, but similar to Gors Fawr circle in Dyfed – was there communication between Wales and Dartmoor at that time? This area remained a sacred site over a very long period, just as Stonehenge and Avebury did; later Bronze Age cairn-circles and stone rows are associated with the stone circle. One of these cairns, excavated in the 1890s, contained a fine beaker, a bronze dagger, a lignite button and a flint knife.

Above: FERNWORTHY, THE SACRED CIRCLE 1907 58486

55

THE CLAPPER BRIDGE   *Postbridge, Devon*

POSTBRIDGE, THE CLAPPER BRIDGE 1907 5788

Clapper bridges had to be strong, as heavy rain on the moor can cause the rivers to rise by three or four feet, turning them into impassable torrents. In this photograph, the East Dart looks like a gentle stream, but in 1890, 1938 and 1992 it has flooded, and its waters have reached or flowed over the bridge, which stands 2m high. However, on each occasion the bridge was undamaged, a tribute to its sturdy design. The local name for the flat slabs which rest on the stone piers is 'posts', hence Postbridge's name. The bridge probably dates from the 14th century, and was built for the benefit of the nearby farms; the first written record of the bridge dates from the 17th century. The granite slabs span nearly 13m; they weigh up to 8 tons each, and must have been brought from nearby tors on sledges dragged by ponies.

Dartmoor's clapper bridges, despite their prehistoric look, are actually medieval; they were constructed for the packhorse trains that were the transport system of the moor.

THE CLAPPER BRIDGE

Dartmeet, Devon

Above left: DARTMEET, THE CLAPPER BRIDGE 1925 78520

Above right: DARTMEET, THE CLAPPER BRIDGE 1925 78521P

Below left: POSTBRIDGE, THE CLAPPER BRIDGE C1955 P102005

BETSY GRIMBÁL'S TOWER — *Tavistock, Devon*

TAVISTOCK, BETSY GRIMBAL'S TOWER, THE ENTRANCE AND A STONE COFFIN 1893 32130

This tower is in fact part of what little remains of the once splendid Tavistock Abbey, founded by Ordgar, Earl of Devon in AD961. The abbey was sacked by the Vikings in AD997 – it was largely destroyed and had to be rebuilt. The tower dates from the 15th century, and represents the west gatehouse of the abbey and part of the abbot's lodging. History does not appear to tell us who Betsy Grimbal was. The stone sarcophagus is said to have contained the bones of Ordulf, Earl of Devon and son of Ordgar; apparently the size of the bones indicated that he had been enormously tall.

Cream tea, pilgrim?

TAVISTOCK, EARL ORDULF'S TOMB 1893 32135

It was Ordulf who undertook the rebuilding of the abbey after it was destroyed by the Vikings. Recent research has discovered that he and his workers were refreshed by the grateful monks with bread, clotted cream and strawberry preserves. This snack was so popular that the monks continued to serve it to travellers. Could this be the origin of the universally popular Devon cream tea?

PIXIES' CROSS

Tavistock, Devon

TAVISTOCK, PIXIES' CROSS AND WHITCHURCH DOWN 1893   32143P

This ancient cross is one of many that marked the route of the old monastic track linking the abbeys of Tavistock and Buckfastleigh. It is said that the monks erected the crosses to make the route visible in bad weather – this was beneficial not only to the monks but to merchants and other travellers as well.

59

THE JUDGE'S CHAIR   *Dunnabridge, Devon*

THE DEWERSTONE *Shaugh Prior, Devon*

OLD CROSS *Harford, Devon*

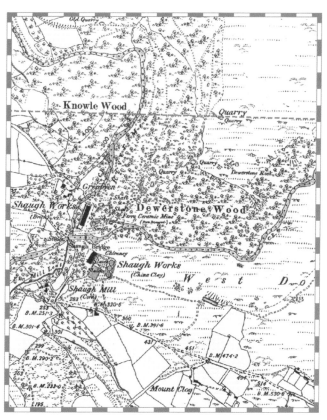

The origins of the Judge's Chair (62315, opposite), sometimes also called the Druid's Chair, are vague. One story is that it was made of slabs taken from the old Stannary Parliament at Crockern Tor, three miles away. William Crossing, in his 'Guide to Dartmoor' (1909), suggests that it is a dolmen, or remains of a neolithic tomb – the wall of the pound behind the Judge's Chair was built on the line of an ancient enclosure.

This little outcrop (S365001, above left) is on the hilltop above the Dewerstone itself, a magnificent 170ft granite sentinel which rises from the steep, wooded hillside above the Plym. The name is a reference to the devil, who is supposed to ride across the cliffs in the dead of night – hence one of the buttresses being named Devil's Rock.

The granite cross in H237022p (above right), 1.35m tall, was once a waymarker on the Abbots' Way that skirts the southern edge of Dartmoor, the ancient track between Buckfast Abbey and Plympton Priory. The cross was discovered in Harford relatively recently; it was being used as a gatepost – a fate not uncommon for these handy-sized pieces of stone. The cross was moved into the churchyard for safekeeping in 1909. It is thought that the cross originally stood not far from where it was found to guide walkers from the moor to the village lane.

Opposite: DARTMOOR, THE JUDGE'S CHAIR, DUNNABRIDGE 1910   62315

Above left: SHAUGH PRIOR, THE ROCKY OUTCROP ABOVE THE DEWERSTONE C1960   S356001

Above right: HARFORD, THE ANCIENT CROSS AND THE MOORS C1960   H237022P

THE LOGAN STONE

Rippon Tor, Devon

There used to be several of these improbably-balanced natural rock formations on Dartmoor. They could be rocked to and fro quite easily, and this one was known as the Nutcracker. It fell prey to vandals in the 1970s. William Crossing, in his 'Guide to Dartmoor' of 1909, wrote of this stone:

'It is called the Nutcrackers, having been the resort of the common people during the nut season, for the purpose of cracking their nuts. That the author in question should have believed that the country people took the trouble to bring nuts to Rippon Tor in order to crack them is certainly surprising, but that he did not tell us the Druids did likewise is much more so. But he may have suspected that these ancient seers preferred to crack jokes, and that the only nuts they cared anything about were chestnuts.'

DARTMOOR, THE LOGAN STONE, RIPPON TOR C1871 5799

THE PIXIES' CAVE *Chudleigh, Devon*

This cave, in the south face of Chudleigh Rock, was used in prehistoric times, but is now the protected home of Greater Horseshoe bats. Today there is a grille over the entrance in the interests of safety – a far cry from the days when local children would show tourists around by candlelight. The cave was traditionally supposed to be the home of Devonshire fairies, or pixies. Inside the cave are many subterranean passages, stalactites and stalagmites.

The Popes' Head stalagmite and pixies' tricks

One particular stalagmite in the Pixies' Cave, which has grown in a round form, is known as the Pope's Head, and in former times was regarded as the guardian of the cavern. The custom used to be to stick pins in the Pope's Head to gain protection from any tricks played upon visitors by the pixies – an example of the folklore tradition that fairies and pixies fear iron.

Left: CHUDLEIGH, THE PIXIES' CAVE 1907 58496
Above: CHUDLEIGH, THE PIXIES' CAVE 1907 58497

THE VIKING BOAT

Exmouth, Devon

This re-enactment of the Viking invasion of Exmouth commemorated one of the earliest events in Exmouth's history. In 1001 the Danish King Sweyn landed with a considerable force, burning and sacking Exmouth before defeating the Saxon army at nearby Pinhoe. There have been several re-enactments in recent years.

Above:
EXMOUTH, THE VIKING
BOAT c1955 E52029

EXMOOR, TARR STEPS 1929 82159AP

This curious prehistoric clapper bridge in a wild and romantic setting serves as a crossing place over the River Barle. The entire structure is 180ft long and has 17 openings or arches. Nothing but the weight of the stones, some of which are over 7ft long, holds them in place. According to a local legend, they were set in place by the devil to win a bet.

Photograph 82159Ap was taken from the opposite side of the river to photograph 82158 (overleaf). To the right, the river is quite shallow normally, so that wheeled vehicles and horses not happy on the stone slabs can ford the river. The Barle can flood violently, and the bridge was washed away in 1947, 1950 and 1980. The slabs are now numbered so that they can be retrieved and replaced in the correct order.

The great planks, flecked with lichen at the edges, are not all level

'Some of the trout came up from under Torre-steps, a singular structure which here connects the shores of the stream. Everyone has seen a row of stepping stones across a shallow brook; now pile other stones on each of these, forming buttresses, and you have the plan of the primitive bridge. It has a megalithic appearance, as if associated with the age of rude stone monuments. They say its origins are doubtful; there can be no doubt of the loveliness of the spot. The Barle comes with his natural rush and fierceness under the unhewn stone planking, then deepens, and there overhanging a black pool – for the shadow was so deep as to be black – grew a large bunch of marsh marigolds in fullest flower, the broad golden cups almost resting on the black water. The bridge is not intended for wheels, and though it is as firm as the rock, foot passengers have to look at their steps, as the great planks, flecked with lichen at the edges, are not all level.'

RICHARD JEFFERIES 1887

EXMOOR, TARR STEPS 1929 82158

Inscribed 'Carataci Nepus' ('descendant of Caratacus') – Caratacus (or Caractacus) was a British chieftain who fought against the Roman invaders in the 1st century AD), this stone probably dates from the 6th century, although the letters are Roman, not Celtic. Some authorities say that it is a standing stone from the Bronze Age – possibly a sacred stone marking the head of a stream – that was inscribed in situ many thousands of years later.

Above: EXMOOR, THE CARATACUS STONE, WINSFORD HILL C1960 E51017

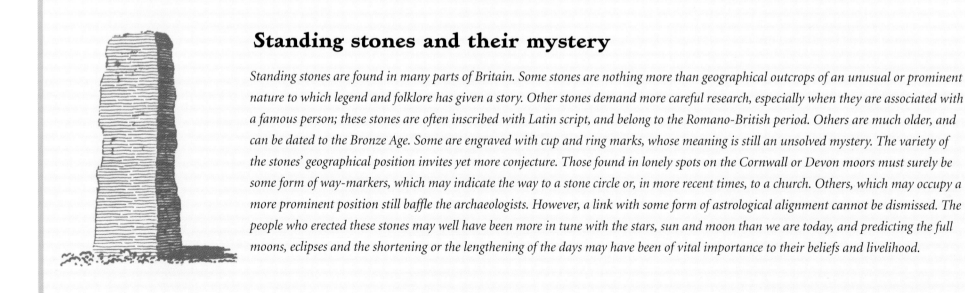

Standing stones and their mystery

Standing stones are found in many parts of Britain. Some stones are nothing more than geographical outcrops of an unusual or prominent nature to which legend and folklore has given a story. Other stones demand more careful research, especially when they are associated with a famous person; these stones are often inscribed with Latin script, and belong to the Romano-British period. Others are much older, and can be dated to the Bronze Age. Some are engraved with cup and ring marks, whose meaning is still an unsolved mystery. The variety of the stones' geographical position invites yet more conjecture. Those found in lonely spots on the Cornwall or Devon moors must surely be some form of way-markers, which may indicate the way to a stone circle or, in more recent times, to a church. Others, which may occupy a more prominent position still baffle the archaeologists. However, a link with some form of astrological alignment cannot be dismissed. The people who erected these stones may well have been more in tune with the stars, sun and moon than we are today, and predicting the full moons, eclipses and the shortening or the lengthening of the days may have been of vital importance to their beliefs and livelihood.

THE TRISCOMBE STONE
Crowcombe, Somerset

CROWCOMBE, THE TRISCOMBE STONE 1898 40347

High on the hill above Crowcombe lies the Triscombe Stone. Some believe it is a wishing stone, but others warn that the Devil musters his spectral Yeth hounds and horsemen there. They chase across the moors in a frantic hunt, and to see or even hear the hounds means certain death. The Yeth, or Wish, hounds of Dartmoor are probably a vestige of folklore belief related to the Wild Hunt of Norse mythology. Woden (to the Anglo-Saxons) or Odin (to the Danes) was believed to chase across the sky on stormy nights with his baying hounds, searching for people to carry off to a distant land. The idea was continued into the Christian tradition, with the Devil replacing Odin, and the hounds searching for the souls of unbaptised babies.

67

Cheddar Gorge is a Site of Special Scientific Interest situated in an Area of Outstanding Natural Beauty, and abounds with rare flora and fauna. The famous caves and rock shelters at Cheddar were inhabited in Upper Palaeolithic and early Mesolithic times, between about 25,000BC and 12,000BC. When the Romantic artistic and literary movement made it fashionable to visit sites of natural splendour, Cheddar with its gorge and caves became one of the most popular tourist attractions in England.

Cheddar Man

The oldest complete skeleton in Britain, 'Cheddar Man' (a young man buried about 8,000BC), was discovered in Cheddar Gorge in 1903; in 1997 it was found that Cheddar Man's DNA matched that of a living descendant – a male teacher at the nearby Kings of Wessex Community School.

Above left: CHEDDAR, THE VILLAGE C1873 6982

Above: CHEDDAR, HIGH ROCKS C1873 6984

Opposite: CHEDDAR, COX'S CAVE C1955 C71037

Without doubt, Cheddar Gorge (opposite) is the most spectacular natural phenomenon in south-west England. The gorge cuts its way out of the carboniferous limestone; it is actually an underground cavern whose roof has collapsed, leaving soaring cliffs and crags of unsurpassed grandeur. Note the Frith photographer's dwarfed carriage in photograph 6984 waiting patiently far below! Discovered in 1837 by George Cox, the cave shown in C71037 (above) is a small, colourful cave with calcite formations of stalactites and stalagmites, pools of water and narrow passages.

Situated at the foot of the southern slope of the Mendips, these caves were named after the village of Wookey, about two miles away. Workmen digging here in 1857 found Stone Age flint tools and the bones of mammoths, hyenas, rhinoceri and lions. In 1912 the archaeologist Herbert Balch excavated the caves, and in the first chamber he found evidence of occupation from the late Iron Age to post-Roman times; he also found the bones of two goats. The first guided tour of the caves was in 1703, but in 1702 the poet Alexander Pope had already shot down a number of beautiful stalactites to decorate the grotto at his home. The caves were formed about 400 million years ago by the rainwater boring through the limestone. The underground streams and lakes, which swirled around to form caverns, finally emerge as the River Axe. A tunnel was opened in 1975 to permit the public to visit previously inaccessible chambers, and modern divers have explored as far as Chamber 25. The caves contain the deepest sump in Britain, at 67m deep.

Storing Cheddar's famous cheese

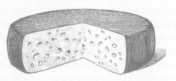

The temperature in the Wookey Hole caves is a constant 11 degrees Celsius – perfect for storing locally made Cheddar cheese (from Wyke Farms, near Bruton), which has been stored here since February 2002. It is believed to be the only cave-matured Cheddar in the country.

Legend says that a witch, exorcised by a monk from Glastonbury Abbey, turned to stone when the monk prayed and threw blessed water over her, and this rock formation is supposed to be her. As with so many old tales, a basis of truth to the story has been unearthed: in his excavations of 1912, Herbert Balch found the skeleton of an old woman, together with a dagger and a polished alabaster ball.

WOOKEY HOLE   *Wookey, Somerset*

Above: WOOKEY HOLE, 'THE WITCH' 1896   38939

Above: WOOKEY HOLE, THE CAVE, THE LAKE AND THE ISLAND 1896   38941

GLASTONBURY TOR

Glastonbury, Somerset

GLASTONBURY, THE TOR 1890 23918

Glastonbury lies in eastern Somerset, set in the Somerset Levels, an area which, until modern drainage methods were used, was marshy and prone to flooding. These conditions led to the formation of layers of peat, which has preserved archaeological remains that do not survive elsewhere – materials such as wood and leather. Important archaeological sites locally include the Iron Age lake villages near Glastonbury and a number of prehistoric trackways.

Glastonbury Tor rises like a cone from the Levels. As a landmark the Tor is enhanced considerably by the tower on its summit, all that remains of a 13th-century church dedicated to the archangel Michael. In legend, Glastonbury has been linked with King Arthur's Isle of Avalon, reminding us that in the past, when the area was even more prone to flooding than it is today, the Tor must have looked like an island in the Levels. Even today, on a winter's morning when the Tor looms above a landscape wreathed in mist, it is hard not to feel affected by a sense of timeless mystery.

Archaeologists have found evidence of occupation on the Tor in prehistory and during the Roman period. There was also occupation in the centuries after the Romans left; was this a defended civil settlement, perhaps the stronghold of a local chieftain? It seems more likely that it was a monastic site pre-dating Glastonbury's abbey, perhaps a hermitage or a retreat. After the abbey was founded in the early 8th century, the Tor continued to be used by hermits – the church of St Michael was built in the 13th century as a pilgrims' chapel.

There are many legends about Glastonbury Tor. One says that it is the home of the Faery King, and that the top of the Tor is a strong focus for faery magic, where visions may be seen. Another, based in Celtic mythology, says that the Tor is a hollow hill, one of the entrances to the Underworld, and the home of the Lord of the Underworld, Gwyn ap Nudd. There is also a possibility that the Tor was encircled by a spiralling, processional way, used in the distant past by priests and priestesses to reach the summit for their rituals. However fanciful these theories, there is sound evidence that the Tor must have had some strong mystical significance in ancient times. The dedication of the church on the Tor to St Michael (38383, right), the archangel who defeated the dragon (symbolic of the Devil), shows that Christians saw the Tor as a site of great pagan significance which needed the protection of their most powerful saint.

The Glastonbury bronze bowl

BRONZE BOWL, ABOUT 2,000 YEARS OLD.

Found on the site of the Prehistoric Lake Village, at Godney, near Glastonbury.

REGISTERED No. 333891.

COPIES IN SILVER AND BRONZE CAN BE OBTAINED OF

FRANKLIN & HARE, PARADE, TAUNTON,

who are, by exclusive permission of the Glastonbury Antiquarian Society,
THE SOLE AUTHORIZED MAKERS.

GLASTONBURY, A BRONZE BOWL C1892 23906A

This is an interesting historical document, and an early example of the commercial exploitation of archaeology. The bronze object that was being copied by this Taunton company is known as the Glastonbury Bowl, and is still considered one of the most important artefacts from the Glastonbury Lake Village. This settlement was discovered by Arthur Bulleid in 1892, and he excavated it over the next 11 years. Between four and a dozen families lived in round houses on a partly artificial island in the swampy wetland between about 250BC and 50BC.

GLASTONBURY, ST MICHAEL'S TOWER 1896 38383

It has been suggested that Glastonbury's abbey might date from the time of Romano-British Christianity before Somerset was conquered by the Saxons; however, it is generally thought that it was founded by King Ine of Wessex in the early 8th century. The most influential person in the early development of the abbey was Dunstan, born nearby at Baltonsborough, who was the abbot from AD940 to AD956. He extended the buildings and reformed the monks' lifestyle with the introduction of the rule of St Benedict. In 1184 fire destroyed most of the building, and almost the whole complex had to be rebuilt. The date of rebuilding is usually given as 1186, although in reality it must have been spread over several years. The abbey grew increasingly wealthy, and was one of the main targets of Henry VIII when he dissolved the monasteries in the 1530s.

Violence on the Tor

During Henry VIII's Dissolution of the Monasteries, the Tor was the site where the last Abbot of Glastonbury, Richard Whiting, and two fellow monks were hanged, drawn and quartered for 'treason' – they resisted Henry's changes.

The story of the 'discovery' of the grave of King Arthur and Queen Guinevere in the abbey grounds in 1191 is now believed to have been a medieval publicity stunt to draw in pilgrims, perhaps to help fund the rebuilding programme after the fire of 1184. Another theory has been put forward by the archaeologist Francis Pryor, in his 'Britain AD' (2004): the discovery was a political scheme encouraged by Henry II and Richard I to appropriate the charisma and influence of King Arthur to the Anglo-Norman rulers – the Arthurian legends had hitherto been centred on Wales.

Above: GLASTONBURY, FROM CHALICE HILL 1912 64472
Left: GLASTONBURY, THE ABBEY, THE TRANSEPT ARCHES
1912 64486P

There is a legend that Joseph of Arimathea, in whose tomb Jesus was laid after the crucifixion, came to Glastonbury as a trader; the Glastonbury Thorn (64488, left) is said to have sprung from Joseph's staff on Wearyall Hill. The thorn bushes in the abbey and others around the town are traditionally descended from the original bush. Although the species of thorn is indeed one that grows in the Holy Land, it is now thought that this legend was concocted around the 13th century by the monks of Glastonbury Abbey in order to encourage pilgrims, and that the original thorn was probably brought back by a crusader. Whatever the truth of the Holy Thorn story may be, a sprig of thorn is presented to the Queen each Christmas.

The well in 61548 (left) was rediscovered when the crypt of the abbey was cleared in 1825. It is thought to be pre-Norman; the Norman arch over it was probably originally a window in the main body of the Lady Chapel of the abbey, and was then set here when later building work made it superfluous. Today the well is only visible from the side, so this photograph offers a better view than the present-day visitor gets.

Above: GLASTONBURY ABBEY, THE HOLY THORN
1912 64488

Left: GLASTONBURY ABBEY, THE HOLY WELL
1909 61548

THE ROMAN BATHS *Bath, Somerset*

The Roman town of Aquae Sulis, now Bath, grew up at the point where the Fosse Way crossed the River Avon. The name indicates that the waters were sacred to the native goddess Sul, whom the Romans identified with Minerva. The temple the Romans built was therefore dedicated to the goddess Sul-Minerva. The town had as its focus the hot spring-fed baths, where citizens of the Roman Empire flocked for rheumatic cures. The Roman baths were sumptuous, and the remains give some idea of their scale and quality. The Great Bath was originally built in the 1st century AD. The flat bottom is lined with 45 sheets of Mendip lead. It is still fed by hot mineral waters from a continuous spring; it is hard to imagine that the water seen today fell as rain on the Mendip Hills 10,000 years ago. In 1897 the architect John Brydon added dignified colonnades around the baths with balustrades and statues. Ever since, visitors have been heard to comment on the remarkable survival of so much original Roman work!

The wonderful pediment from the temple of Sul-Minerva (57725, below), carved in Bath stone, portrays the famous Gorgon's Head. The carving has Celtic and Roman features, and was part of a sculptured shield. Today its real meaning is not clear, since the head, though closely similar to the female Gorgon, is male with flowing hair and blazing eyes, and has similarities with the sea-gods Oceanus and Neptune. It was found in 1790 below the Pump Room.

Above: BATH, THE ROMAN BATHS, THE SCULPTURE FROM THE TEMPLE OF SUL-MINERVA 1907 57725

Right: BATH, THE ROMAN BATHS 1890 25135P

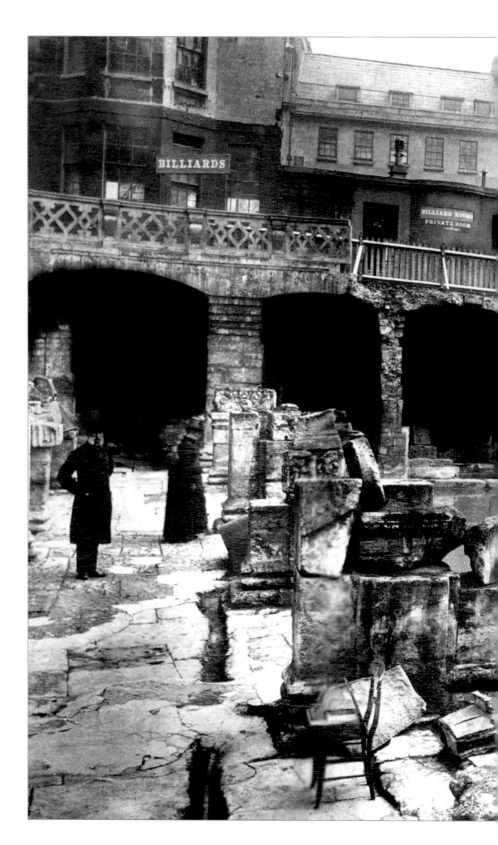

THE HUNDRED STONE

Yeovil, Somerset

YEOVIL, THE HUNDRED STONE 2004 Y11708K

Under laws made by the Anglo-Saxon King Alfred the Great, the country was divided into shires and the legal and administrative affairs were dealt with by a shire court, or moot. Each division was made up to contain a hundred families, and these in turn were divided into tithings, ten householders living close together, and bound over as sureties for each other's peaceable behaviour. Legal business would be carried out at formal gatherings held every three to four weeks. These were more often than not conducted in the open air, allegedly from the fear of spirits said to be lurking in the walls of buildings. Yeovil's meetings were held around the Hundred Stone, which can still be seen today at a crossroads on the highest point in Mudford Road, a perfect spot for looking over the plain towards the Mendips and Glastonbury.

The very last meeting at the Yeovil Hundred Stone was in 1843, when a bailiff, two constables, and tithingmen were appointed. After a customary offering of port had been poured on the stone, the meeting adjourned to a local pub for dinner.

HAMBLEDON HILL   *Child Okeford, Dorset*

Above: CHILD OKEFORD, HAMBLEDON HILL
C1960   C222014

Many of the obvious landmarks that command our attention in the British countryside are the Iron Age hill-forts. At Hambledon Hill the Iron Age builders skilfully engineered three massive tiers of ramparts to follow the long, sinuous shape of the hill, which overlooks the Blackmore Vale – it is a landmark for miles around. Inside the ramparts, which enclose an area of about 12.5 hectares, it is still possible to see many platforms on which huts were built.

But Hambledon Hill has an impressively long history. Many hundreds of years before the hill-fort was constructed, two causewayed camps and two long barrows were built here during the middle Neolithic era. Causewayed camps are so called because the banks and ditches surrounding the enclosure are broken up with gaps in between, presumably to allow access. Their purpose remains in general a mystery, but they could have been ritual sites, market places, or corrals for livestock.

The massive Neolithic complex on Hambledon Hill was extensively excavated in the 1970s and 1980s, and was radio-carbon dated to 2,900–2,600BC. Excavations at one of the causewayed camps revealed that the ditch contained many human bones. The skeletons were disarticulated, implying that the bodies had been exposed and allowed to decompose before being placed in the ditch. There were also some crouched infant burials, and skulls placed at intervals around the enclosure. Within the camp were a number of ritual pits containing offerings such as a greenstone axe and red deer antlers. This enclosure thus appears to have been a large cemetery. It has been estimated that the complex would have taken about 45,000 man-hours to complete – it must have been of great ritual significance.

About 80m south-east of the large camp is another Neolithic enclosure which had a bigger ditch. The large amount of charcoal found here suggests that there was a timber palisade which was attacked and destroyed by fire. An intact skeleton of a man was found at the entrance with a flint-tipped arrow embedded in his chest. More human skulls were found around this enclosure, but in this case the heads appear to have been deliberately severed. As traces of several timber structures were found within this enclosure, it may have been a habitation site.

The archaeological evidence shows that people gathered at both enclosures over a long period of time, long after the camps had been built. They seem to have come to use the sites for ritual feasting on a seasonal system; analysis of the animal bones found here shows that most of the meat consumed came from animals slaughtered in the late summer or autumn.

HOD HILL

Stourpaine, Dorset

Although Hod Hill is not as visually impressive as other Dorset Iron Age hill-forts such as Hambledon Hill and Maiden Castle, the enclosed area within the rectangular fortifications at Hod Hill makes it the largest Iron Age hill-fort in the county. Construction work on the hill-fort was probably begun in the 5th century BC. The interior was packed with hundreds of round-houses and storage pits; the houses appear to have been built following street lines, and traces of the buildings and pits can still be found in the depressions and hollows on the ground, best seen in the south-east corner. The fort appears to have been home to a dense population at the time of the Roman invasion in AD43, when it was overwhelmed by the forces of the future emperor Vespasian and the Second Legion.

Soon after taking the hill-fort, the Romans established an auxiliary camp on the north-west corner of the hill. The Roman fort had three gates, each of which had a watchtower, and there was a fourth tower in the south-east corner. From excavations of the barrack block, it has been calculated that around 600 men and a cavalry unit of 250 could have been garrisoned here. The fort appears to have only been occupied for a short period, and was probably abandoned around AD51. The buildings were apparently destroyed by fire, but whether by attack, accident or deliberate destruction by the outgoing forces we shall never know.

Slings and arrows

The Romans appear to have attacked Hod Hill using their artillery, or ballistas, concentrating their attack on the south-east entrance. Excavations revealed a large concentration of ballista bolts around the largest round-house in the fort, which was surrounded by a palisade and had a pile of sling-stones by its doors. The Durotriges tribe were known to have used slings as an effective weapon, and a large number of sling-stones were also found at Maiden Castle near Dorchester in Dorset.

Above left: STOURPAINE,
THE ROMAN CAMP ON HOD HILL
C1939 S446016

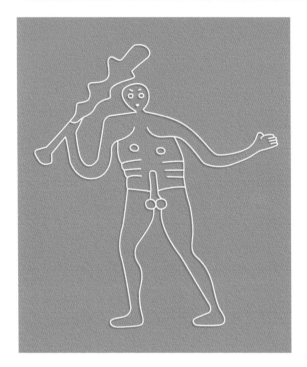

Out of the frying pan

Just above the Giant is an enclosure known as the Frying Pan or Trendle. For many years this was the scene of maypole dancing and Midsummer celebrations, linking the Giant to early memories of fertility rites; it has been noted that the Giant's phallus points directly at the rising sun around May Day. One of the local fertility traditions is that a girl who spends the night sleeping within the outline of the figure will be the mother of many children, and childless couples are still known to visit the Giant.

One of the most famous – and notorious – ancient monuments in Britain is the chalk-cut figure of the Cerne Giant in Dorset, standing 180ft high, often called the Rude Man of Cerne. The figure is of a nude man, with ribs, nipples and phallus accentuated; he holds a club, and may at one time have also held a cloak over his other, outstretched, arm. It is also possible that there was at least one other figure nearby, long since lost under the turf, possibly of a dog. The figure is regularly 'scoured', or cleaned, by local people; every seven years is the standard interval, and the scouring usually takes four men a full day.

Local legend said that the people of Cerne once killed a real giant on the hillside as he lay sleeping off a meal of sheep that he had stolen, and they drew around his outline to commemorate the event. The real origins of the figure remain a mystery, although there are many theories. If the figure really dates from Roman Britain, as many believe, it seems strange that the monks at Cerne Abbey allowed the pagan and immodest figure to remain on the hillside, and it was not mentioned in accounts of the village in 1356 or 1617. However, this may have been for prudish reasons, and there is a strong case for believing that the figure is of some antiquity. One interpretation is that he represents a Celtic god called Nodens, and a bronze handle of Celtic origin has been found elsewhere which features a representation of a naked man very similar in style to the Cerne Giant. The most likely suggestion, originally made by Stukeley in 1764, is that the Giant represents Hercules, and the National Trust uses this interpretation in its handbook. The style of the Giant and his club are typical of Romano-British art, and the Hercules cult was popular at the end of the 2nd century AD. A resistivity test in 1979 showed what appeared to be a lion skin over the Giant's outstretched arm, which provides strong support for the Hercules theory.

THE MINSTER

Wimborne Minster, Dorset

Wimborne's minster church is dedicated to St Cuthberga, who founded a nunnery here in AD705. It gained an international reputation, and in about AD740 sent 30 nuns to Germany to help St Boniface convert the local tribes to Christianity. Healing the sick is the theme of this window in the minster's north-west corner, which shows St Luke (traditionally a doctor himself) with St Cuthberga, the minster's founder.

The oldest of three chests in St George's chapel at Wimborne Minster is thought to date from the time of Wimborne's Saxon monastery and nunnery (see 19480a, page 81). It was hewn from a single log and had no less than six locks, thought at one time to have secured an amazing array of religious relics, which have long since disappeared. These are said to have included pieces of the Lord's cross and manger, some of the ground where Jesus was born, hairs from His beard, part of St Agatha's thigh-bone, one of St Philip's teeth, one of St Cecilia's joints, and St Thomas of Canterbury's hair shirt and some of his blood.

BADBURY RINGS

Wimborne Minster, Dorset

Now a tree-clad hilltop fort with three circular ramparts, Badbury Rings is an example of the many hill-forts built by the Iron Age people. It stands at the junction of two Roman roads, the Ackling Dyke running from Dorchester to Old Sarum, and the Bath to Poole road, although there is still doubt that the latter was ever completed. This is one of the possible sites for the battle of Mount Badon, mentioned in the 10th-century Nennius's 'History of the Britons', when King Arthur (and his forces) killed 960 Saxons in a single day in about AD520 – one of the few references to King Arthur in pre-medieval chronicles.

Above: WIMBORNE MINSTER, BADBURY RINGS C1955 B751042

Right: WIMBORNE MINSTER, THE SAXON CHEST 1886 19480A

Opposite left: WIMBORNE MINSTER, ST LUKE AND ST CUTHBERGA'S WINDOW 1908 60632

MAIDEN CASTLE | *Dorchester, Dorset*

The story of Dorchester as a town only began after the arrival of the Romans. However, the area in and around modern Dorchester contains an outstanding assemblage of prehistoric monuments and landscapes which show that long before the town came into being, this was a well-settled area with considerable spiritual significance. The most impressive and best-known feature is Maiden Castle. This brooding presence just outside the town is one of Britain's largest Iron Age hill-forts.

There are two knolls on Maiden Castle, and around 3,000BC, during the Neolithic period, an enclosure was constructed on the eastern one. After this enclosure was abandoned, a bank barrow (an elongated burial mound) was constructed. There is no evidence of activity here for the next 1,500 years. Then the first phase of the hill-fort's development began around 500BC in the early Iron Age: a bank and ditch were constructed, again on the eastern knoll. These defences were extended around the whole hilltop 250 years later. An additional bank and ditch were added about a century afterwards, and there was further strengthening between 100BC and 75BC.

The hill-fort's defences are still spectacular today, even after over 2,000 years of erosion, but when first constructed they would have been even more impressive: the chalk subsoil would have been exposed in the ditch sides, and there would have been a lot of upcast chalk in the banks – this would have gleamed white in sunlight, and made the fortifications visible from many points between the Ridgeway to the south and the edge of the chalk downs across the middle of Dorset.

Above:
DORCHESTER,
MAIDEN CASTLE,
THE EARTH-
WORKS C1950
D44008

Right:
DORCHESTER,
MAIDEN CASTLE
1913   65617

John Byng on the age of Maiden Castle

*The 18th-century traveller John Byng did not realise how old Maiden Castle is:
'I bent my course to Maiden Castle, a Roman fortification overlooking the town
of Dorchester; I traversed every part, and believe it to be the most perfect vestige
of the Romans in England; the fosses are all perfect; it must have been strong and
a work of great labour ... I have always been puzzled to conceive how, in such
situations, they could furnish themselves with provisions and water but at an
amazing risk.'*

JOHN BYNG, 'RIDES ROUND BRITAIN' 1782

There is no evidence for other settlements in the area during the early phases of Maiden Castle's development in the Iron Age, which indicates that most of the local population were living within the hill-fort; but during the later Iron Age, settlements outside the hill-fort reappeared, and the area that was occupied within the hill-fort decreased. Hence the theory (favoured by Sir Mortimer Wheeler and his contemporaries in the 1930s) that at the time of the Roman invasion Maiden Castle was the political centre of the local tribe, the Durotriges, is in some doubt.

In AD44 the hill-fort was taken by the Second Augustan Legion, commanded by Vespasian (later to become emperor). Excavations have revealed 54,000 sling-stones, which in the end were inadequate weapons against Roman technology, discipline and experience. One of the most poignant exhibits in the excellent Dorset County Museum in Dorchester is the skeleton of one of the British defenders of Maiden Castle with a ballista bolt from the Roman artillery embedded in his spine.

Dorchester, Dorset

DORCHESTER, THE ROMAN AMPHITHEATRE 1922 72756

The Roman amphitheatre at Maumbury Rings is unique. Although its setting is difficult to appreciate today because of houses and other buildings around it, Maumbury Rings is set on a prominent ridge – probably a deliberate choice by its first builders. An archaeological excavation of the monument took place from 1908 to 1913. It found that the feature had first been constructed as a henge monument in the late Neolithic period around 2,500BC. There was a ditch inside the bank, and a single entrance at the north where a standing stone was placed. Within the ditch, at intervals of 3m, there were shafts whose bases were on average 10.4m below ground level.

In the 1st century AD, Maumbury Rings was converted into an amphitheatre, quite possibly by the Roman army unit that was probably stationed close by. The interior was lowered by 3m to make an arena, with the excavated material being added to the bank, which became the spectators' viewing area. The entrance remained in the same place, but a ramp was now necessary to reach the lowered internal surface. A passageway with a timber wall on either side ran around the arena, and this had three rooms along it, for changing rooms, or for letting out animals or combatants, perhaps. Cockfighting, animal baiting, and the like were probably the main entertainments, with gladiatorial fights being rare events, particularly in a new province without the facilities to train the combatants. The amphitheatre continued in use, presumably by the townsfolk, after the fort was abandoned, then went out of use around the middle of the 2nd century, before a revival from the mid 3rd to the mid 4th centuries. The amphitheatre is still used now for staging outdoor theatrical performances.

DORCHESTER, THE ROMAN EXCAVATIONS 1939   D44003

THE ROMAN EXCAVATIONS

Dorchester, Dorset

Beneath present-day Dorchester lie the remains of the extensive Roman town of Durnovaria. The number of discoveries of luxurious houses, many with mosaic floors, in Dorchester attests to the wealth of some of the inhabitants. The Roman town house in the grounds of County Hall is a good example, and it is thought to be the only excavation of a complete urban Roman house on display in Britain. The excavations were carried out in 1937 and 1938. The house was sited in the north-west corner of the Roman defences; this was otherwise an industrial area. The first phase, of the later 2nd to early 3rd centuries AD, had only timber buildings. Then in the late 3rd century the house was rebuilt in stone, and it continued to be added to, perhaps by different generations of the same family. The west range was the main living area, and it included mosaic floors and at least one glazed window – glass was an expensive material then. The south range contained a more utilitarian suite of rooms. Both ranges had under-floor hypocaust heating systems in one of the rooms. The building was largely abandoned at the time of the breakdown of Roman authority around the early 5th century.

When the significance of the discovery of the Roman town house was recognised, the plans for the new County Hall were changed so that the house could be preserved. After the excavation, the remains were left open to the elements, as we see in D44001. The site became a visitor attraction (the people in the photograph are looking at the west range), but the weather and the feet of the visitors had a detrimental effect on the remains, particularly the mosaics. Dorset County Council had intended to construct a covering building, but the Second World War began and priorities changed. The remains were left uncovered until about 1950, when the upstanding walls were consolidated and the mosaics covered with turf to protect them. One mosaic alone could still be seen, covered by a small shed-like structure. In the 1990s the County Council decided to redisplay the site. The mosaics of the western range were uncovered and conserved and a cover building was built over that range. This was designed to give an impression of the original Roman building while being recognisably modern.

DORCHESTER, THE ROMAN EXCAVATIONS 1939   D44001

DORCHESTER, THE REMAINS OF THE HYPOCAUST 1939 D44006

Below we see a close-up of one of the mosaics in the Roman town house. Archaeologists have analysed many of the mosaics found in this country; after studying the different designs, they have concluded that there were distinct 'schools' of mosaic makers working in certain places and using their own styles. One such school is thought to have been based in Dorchester (hence its name, the Durnovaria school), and it was responsible for most of the mosaics in the town and the surrounding countryside. The materials used for the mosaics were not imported; local (and thus cheaper) materials were exploited. In Dorchester, for instance, chalk and limestone from nearby quarries were used, as well as broken shards of pottery.

DORCHESTER, A TESSELLATED PAVEMENT, THE ROMAN EXCAVATIONS 1939 D44004

In the Dorset County Museum in Dorchester, there are three mosaics set into the floor. Visitors sometimes express surprise that they can walk on such Roman artefacts – but this is what they were designed for! The last floor was lifted and placed in the museum in 1927. According to the information plaque next to the floor, it has been called 'the death of Thomas Hardy'. The elderly author, who lived just outside the town, left his sickbed to see it and died three months later, his condition presumably aggravated by the effort.

In the Roman town house in the grounds of County Hall there is evidence of squatter occupation from the last years of Roman administration or soon after. Fires were lit directly on the mosaics, a well was dug into the floor of one of the rooms, and there is even evidence of deliberate vandalism of the mosaic floors.

DORCHESTER, THE ROMAN WALL 2004 D44716K

In the later 2nd century AD, Durnovaria acquired defences. This reflected a period of uncertainty, perhaps civil war. As well as protecting against invaders from outside the Empire, these defences may also have been intended to keep out the Roman army – some soldiers were not averse to the occasional mutiny and outbreak of looting.

At Durnovaria, a rampart with an outer ditch was constructed around a roughly square area that is today largely followed by the Walks, although part of the route on the north side beside the river is not known for certain. The rampart was generally constructed of alternate layers of earth and chalk, much of which was undoubtedly the material excavated from the ditches, perhaps supplemented by material brought from quarry pits nearby. There was also a counterscarp bank, a smaller bank outside the ditch, for extra defence. At the gates into the town, there may also have been more complex arrangements of banks and ditches. Then in the 4th century the defences were strengthened by the addition of a wall to the top of the rampart.

Although most of the circuit of the Roman defences of Dorchester can still be followed, only one short section of the original wall survives. When most of the walls were deliberately levelled in the 18th century, the part we see in D44716k (above), on West Walks near Top o' Town roundabout, survived because it was a property boundary. Only the core of the wall survives (the original facing stones are missing), and it has perhaps been partly reconstructed.

THE WISHING WELL *Upwey, Dorset*

UPWEY, THE WISHING WELL C1897 34554AP

'Long before Christianity ever came to England our forebears showed their reverence for water and it is not hard to imagine the awe in which they would have held the powerful, silent surge that we later came to know as Upwey's Wishing Well. How natural, then, that in pagan times the whole area would have been thought holy and that with the coming of Christianity … a chapel should have been built on it.' FROM THE GUIDEBOOK TO ST LAURENCE'S CHURCH, UPWEY

It is said that in Saxon times the spring at Upwey was renowned for its healing powers. George III, whose visits made nearby Weymouth a fashionable watering place, often came here to take the waters. A special gold cup was kept for him to use – the cup was later presented to Royal Ascot as a trophy. Later, in Victorian times, the spring became a successful commercial enterprise by becoming a wishing well. Two village ladies (is that one of them on the left in the above photograph?) were employed to hand out glasses and encourage visitors to wish – and to pay for the privilege! The little arched building was erected in 1887 to commemorate Queen Victoria's Golden Jubilee.

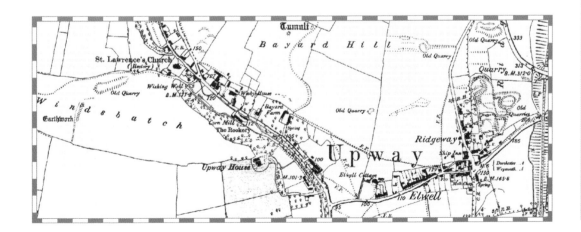

Top: UPWEY, THE WISHING WELL 1898   41131

A curious spectacle for the twentieth century ...

'The village of Upwey – the Upper Town on the Wey – affords an extraordinary instance of the value of a happy, if meaningless, title. Upwey is one of the places of pilgrimage for the Weymouth holiday-makers. They come here in hundreds, mostly in coaches and wagonettes. The reason for their coming to Upwey is a spring there with the fascinating title of the "Wishing Well". It is to see the Wishing Well that the romantically minded pay their shillings for a seat in the crowded char-a-banc.

The well, as I remember it some forty years ago, was a spot of faint interest; its powers were ill-defined, and there was no particular ground for assuming that a wish expressed at Upwey would have especial advantage. The place is pleasant enough, in spite of the crowd, the swings, and the tea-gardens. A spring issues from the foot of a wooded bank, and, hurrying away under an avenue of trees, vanishes at the mill. A seat placed under two ridiculous stone arches has been erected for the benefit of the tripper. For the benefit of the villager, on the other hand, the following ritual has been introduced, which has proved to be more lucrative than a mere gazing at the waters.

The wisher receives a glass of water from the custodian of this Fons Bandusea, he drinks it with appropriate giggling, empties the glass by throwing the water over his left shoulder, and, most important of all, makes an offering of money to the keeper of the well. Folk of all kind go through this formula for the attaining of supposed ends – old men and maidens, young men and children. It is a curious spectacle for the twentieth century even if it serves no more than to illustrate the magic of a pleasing name.'

'HIGHWAYS AND BYWAYS OF DORSET', JOSEPH PENNELL, 1914

IRON AGE LOG BOAT — *Poole, Dorset*

POOLE, AN IRON AGE LOGBOAT IN THE WATERFRONT MUSEUM 2004 P72701K

In August 1964 a dredger working off Brownsea Island in Poole Harbour made an important archaeological discovery. The long wooden object that was found preserved in a layer of peat in Brownsea Roads turned out to be part of a canoe that had been hewn out of a huge oak trunk. A diver later recovered a second section. Put together, the two pieces indicate that the vessel measured 33ft from stern to prow, 4ft at its widest point, and had a draught of about 12 inches. Radio-carbon dating has since dated the Poole logboat to 295BC, give or take 50 years. Its shallow draught made it ideally suited to a harbour which has an average depth of only 2ft 6 inches today and is thought to have been even shallower 2,300 years ago. The flat-bottomed 'Poole punt' used by today's fishermen has been described as a direct descendant of the logboat.

Even more recently, in 2002, archaeologists made another discovery, which has led to Poole being described as Britain's oldest known cross-Channel port. The remains of two jetties extending from Green Island and Cleavel Point on the south side of the harbour provide evidence that there was a flourishing port here 200 years before the Roman invasion. 'Timber pilings excavated from a deep layer of silt on the sea bed have been radio-carbon dated at 250BC, the oldest substantial port structures by several centuries anywhere on the British coast,' reported the Guardian on 17 September 2002. 'They suggest an Iron Age trading complex, with massive stone and timber jetties reaching out into the deep water channel, providing berths for the largest ocean going ships - raising the possibility of Greek and Roman traders making the journey from the Mediterranean to the Dorset coast. The scale of the construction work was astounding, and implied a large, skilled and organised workforce. Two jetties have been traced, one with a surviving length of 45 metres but probably originally the same length as the other 80-metre jetty. The surface was eight metres across, and smooth paved with shaped flagstones. The jetties were built up from an estimated 10,000 tonnes of rock and rubble, reinforced with hundreds of oak tree trunks, sharpened at one end so they could be rammed into the sea bed.'

THE OLD ROMAN BRIDGE

The New Forest, Hampshire

A Roman road ran through the New Forest, which was of great use commercially to the Romans. The area supplied wood and charcoal to fire kilns for the manufacture of pottery or the smelting of iron. It is said that this bridge (60124, left) was used by the Romans.

Left: THE NEW FOREST, THE OLD ROMAN BRIDGE 1908 60124

WINCHESTER, KING ALFRED'S STATUE 1901   43677A

King Alfred (AD849–899), the only English monarch to be termed 'the Great', became ruler of the West Saxons after the death of his brother Ethelred in AD871. He is noted not only as a great warrior who defeated and made peace with the Danes, but also as a devout scholar and social reformer. He built new fortified towns, or 'burhs', and established an improved legal system, limiting the practice of blood feud and imposing heavy penalties for breach of oath. He set great store by learning and education; he founded schools and promoted learning, as well as restoring the country's defences and building up an improved navy to meet future Danish attacks. Winchester was one of his burhs, and became Alfred's capital city. After his death he was buried at the Old Minster there, but his remains were later moved to Hyde Abbey. This photograph shows the splendid bronze statue that was fashioned by Hamo Thornycroft to commemorate the 1,000th anniversary of Alfred's death in AD899, and which was unveiled in 1901. The statue stands at the site of the old East Gate into Alfred's burh.

The Alfred Jewel

This famous object was found in 1693 near the site of Athelney Abbey in Somerset. It is now kept in the Ashmolean Museum in Oxford. Alfred knew Somerset well; he retreated to the area around Athelney in AD878 to regroup his forces during his long struggle against the Danes, and after his victory at the Battle of Edington he founded a monastery in the area. The jewel is made of gold and cloisonné enamel. The figure on the jewel has been interpreted as either a representation of Christ as the Wisdom of God, or possibly a personification of Sight. The function of the jewel is unknown, but it may have been one of the 'aestels', or book pointers, which we know that King Alfred sent to each bishopric in his realm with a copy of his own translation of Pope Gregory's 'Pastoral Care'. Alternatively it may have been a symbol of office, possibly sent by Alfred to one of his bishops or officials. The inscription on the jewel in Anglo-Saxon, 'Aelfred mec heht gewyrcan', means 'Alfred ordered me to be made'.

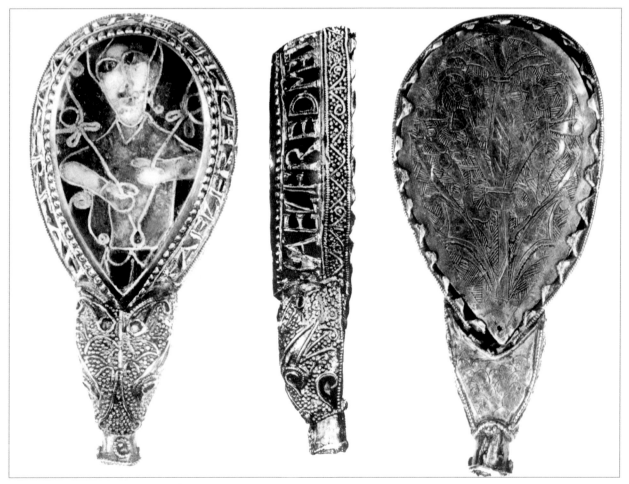

THE ALFRED JEWEL 1907 57416

King Alfred's glorious victory

'The same year, after Easter, King Alfred, with a few followers, made for himself a stronghold in a place called Athelney, and from thence sallied with his vassals and the nobles of Somersetshire, to make frequent assaults upon the pagans. Also, in the seventh week after Easter, he rode to the stone of Egbert, which is in the eastern part of the wood which is called Selwood, which means in Latin Silva Magna, the Great Wood, but in British Coit-mawr. Here he was met by all the neighbouring folk of Somersetshire, and Wiltshire, and Hampshire, who had not, for fear of the pagans, fled beyond the sea; and when they saw the king alive after such great tribulation, they received him, as he deserved, with joy and acclamations, and encamped there for one night. When the following day dawned, the king struck his camp, and went to Okely, where he encamped for one night. The next morning he removed to Edington, and there fought bravely and perseveringly against all the army of the pagans, whom, with the divine help, he defeated with great slaughter, and pursued them flying to their fortification. Immediately he slew all the men, and carried off all the booty that he could find without the fortress, which he immediately laid siege to with all his army; and when he had been there fourteen days, the pagans, driven by famine, cold, fear, and last of all by despair, asked for peace, on the condition that they should give the king as many hostages as he pleased, but should receive none of him in return, in which form they had never before made a treaty with any one. The king, hearing that, took pity upon them, and received such hostages as he chose; after which the pagans swore, moreover, that they would immediately leave the kingdom; and their king, Gothrun, promised to embrace Christianity, and receive baptism at king Alfred's hands.'

'THE LIFE OF KING ALFRED', WRITTEN AD888 BY BISHOP ASSER, TRANSLATION BY DR J A GILES (LONDON 1847)

BRADING, MORTON, THE ROMAN VILLA, THE HYPOCAUST 2005 B175702K

Roman villas, their rectangular design so markedly at odds with the Celtic round-house tradition, were isolated country retreats and farms. This one, overlooking the vast inland waters of Brading Haven at Morton on the Isle of Wight, may have started out soon after the arrival of the Romans in the 1st century as something altogether more modest – the archaeological evidence suggests just a few simple timber buildings – but the site had certainly been dramatically transformed by the beginning of the 4th century. With its buildings grouped around a courtyard, this was now the location for a large, complex farmhouse, clearly the home of someone of considerable importance. It probably remained so until the Roman retreat from Britain in AD410, and then itself retreated into ruin, disappearing beneath the rising ground over the centuries that followed until, finally, it was re-discovered in 1879.

The Morton villa's remains, including the bath block, the ingenious central heating system (which we see in the photograph), frescoes depicting mythical scenes and the magnificent floor mosaics in the preserved west wing, are now among the Island's most famous tourist attractions, managed by the Oglander Roman Trust, which has just constructed a new protective 'over-building' and visitor centre, ending fears that the excavated remains might have to be re-buried in order to protect them from the ravages of exposure.

The Isle of Wight contains about 170 round barrows, which are mostly grouped on the east-west chalk ridge, with a few on the southern chalk country near Ventnor. But tramp along the coastal path across Headon Warren near Alum Bay in the Isle of Wight's far west, and here on the sandy heathland is a good example of a barrow of the Bronze Age, helpfully identified by information panels (A41701k, left). The path has been diverted in recent years around the barrow to safeguard its own diminishing 'roundness' from further obliteration. Along with two smaller barrows in the field below, the Headon mound probably dates from around 1,500BC.

BRONZE AGE BARROW   *Alum Bay, Isle of Wight*

ALUM BAY, THE BRONZE AGE BURIAL MOUND 2005   A41701K

The Bronze Age

The period of around 2,500BC to 750BC is usually referred to as the Bronze Age. Travel and trade spread new and more efficient methods of farming, and also metallurgy. The Bronze Age peoples understood that the mixture of tin and copper produces bronze, and both metals were in abundance in Cornwall. Gold jewellery appeared now for the first time, and is found with burials in the distinctive round burial mounds of these people. Nature, the seasons, fertility and death dominated their beliefs. Perhaps the most outstanding monuments they left were the stone circles that are to be found throughout the whole of the British Isles, the best known of which is Stonehenge. It seems that these were used for funerary and ritual purposes, and some may have had an astronomical or calendar function linked to the agricultural year. The circles range from very small sites, which may have been used by an individual family group or local community, to large complexes like Stonehenge, which can perhaps be seen as the 'cathedrals' of their era.

THE LONG STONE   *Mottistone, Isle of Wight*

MOTTISTONE, THE LONG STONE 2005   M399702K

The Long Stone near Mottistone is the Isle of Wight's oldest landmark relic of human activity, the Island's one surviving man-made Neolithic monument (M399702k, left). What purpose drove those early islanders 5,000 years ago to erect what later generations would call the Long Stone? Various theories have been put forward. Arguably the most plausible is the suggestion that the giant upright stone was one of a pair, possibly with the smaller stone that lies horizontally today at its base, carefully positioned to focus the light of the rising sun into an adjacent long barrow, where the ancestors of those who manoeuvred the stones into position lay buried, and whose spirits would be awakened by the warmth of the sun's rays. It is further suggested that this would have occurred only rarely, possibly on Midwinter's Day, adding further mystique to the monument. What, centuries later, the Anglo-Saxons made of it all, we can but guess, yet it is probable that they recognised this as a site of spiritual importance. It was, according to a widely accepted theory, used as their Moot (or Meeting) Stone, where the Anglo-Saxon elders called men to solemn assembly, and it is a very short step from that to the name now borne by the nearby hamlet and manor house of Mottistone.

PORTCHESTER CASTLE   *Portsmouth, Hampshire*

The Romans built Portchester Castle (Portus Adurni) in the 3rd century AD to defend the English Channel from raiding Saxons, and it is one of the largest of the Saxon Shore forts. The term 'Saxon Shore' ('litus saxonicum') comes from a 4th-century listing of military sites and commands, the Notitia Dignitatum; there were ten Saxon Shore forts, including Brancaster, Reculver, Burgh (see page 155), Dover, and Pevensey. Portchester was garrisoned until the late 3rd century and then again in the mid 4th century when barbarian raids threatened once more. The massive masonry walls still largely survive. They were over 3m wide and 6m high and fronted by ditches, and enclosed buildings and metalled roads – none of these are visible today. 20 D-shaped bastions projected from the walls, of which 14 survive – we can see one of them in P73050. In the 11th century the enclosure was used as the bailey for a Norman castle (30030ap) – the Normans took stone from the Roman fort to build it.

Above: PORTCHESTER CASTLE 1892   30030AP   *Right:* PORTCHESTER CASTLE C1960   P73050

THE SAXON CHURCH — *Corhampton, Hampshire*

One of Hampshire's hidden treasures, this lovely Saxon church lies near the River Meon and has changed little over the years. The sundial on the south wall is divided not into twelve sections, as is usual today, but eight three-hour 'tides', representing the Saxon way of counting time. The wall paintings in the chancel are among the most important in the country, and probably date from the 12th century.

One thing Corhampton has which must set any mind thinking, a sundial which has been here 900 years. Before the Conqueror came people passing through Corhampton would look up at this stone clock on sunny days, and here it is today. Beautifully sculptured leaves radiate from its centre.   ARTHUR MEE, 'THE KING'S ENGLAND: HAMPSHIRE' 1939

Left: CORHAMPTON, THE SAXON CHURCH C1960   C575001

BUTSER ANCIENT FARM

Petersfield, Hampshire

PETERSFIELD, BUTSER ANCIENT FARM 2005   P48721K

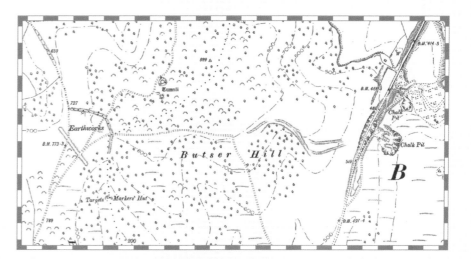

Four miles south of Petersfield in Hampshire, just off the A3, is the Butser Ancient Farm, a replica of the sort of farm which existed during the Iron Age, c300BC. Here it is possible to see the kinds of buildings, structures and occasionally animals, fields and crops which existed at this time. However, it is not only a museum. It prides itself also on being a large open-air laboratory where research is undertaken into the Iron Age and the succeeding Roman period. The design of the replica farm is based soundly on evidence (for instance, ditches, banks, postholes, pits, pottery, pollen and carbonised material) gleaned from archaeological sites. It is the only place in Western Europe where all the ancient varieties of prehistoric wheat can be seen growing in fields.

THE SAXON CHURCH   *Albury, Surrey*

ALBURY, THE SAXON CHURCH 1890   23483

This beautiful Saxon church, recorded in the Domesday Book, once stood in the centre of the old village of Albury. Then in the 19th century the owners of the manor house gradually moved the villagers away to nearby hamlets (the present village of Albury) so as to enlarge their park and gain more privacy. In 1841 Henry Drummond built a new parish church, and the old church was closed and left to decay until 1921. Then the decision was taken to restore the old church; it was packed for the first service held there for 80 years, and the Churches Conservation Trust restored the building and rebuilt the chancel. Inside the church there is a fine wall painting depicting St Christopher and a medieval brass of a knight in armour. Nowadays services are held every year at midsummer and Christmas.

DUNSFOLD, THE HOLY WELL C1955 D68027

THE HOLY WELL

Dunsfold, Surrey

The waters of the holy well of St Mary at Dunsfold were believed to have healing powers, particularly for eye ailments. Tradition says that the Blessed Virgin herself appeared at this spot, which may be why the village church was built near this site, at some distance from the village. The well itself is located in a beautiful spot on the banks of a tributary of the River Arun. The fine canopy, designed by the eminent church architect W D Caroe, was erected in 1933.

Chichester's wonderful medieval market cross dominates the cityscape, positioned as it is at the site where, nearly 2,000 years ago, the east-west and north-south Roman roads intersected in the centre of the walled Roman town of Noviomagus Regnensium. An inscription in the town suggests that this area, occupied by the Regnenses under their ruler Cogidubnus, was a client kingdom of Rome before and just after the occupation; during the 1st century AD a Roman town was built here.

'At the top of the street, into which, with my guide-book, I relapsed, was an old market-cross of the fifteenth century – a florid, romantic little structure. It consists of a stone pavilion, with open sides and a number of pinnacles and crockets and buttresses, besides a goodly medallion of the high-nosed visage of Charles I, which was placed above one of the arches, at the Restoration, in compensation for the violent havoc wrought upon the little town by the Parliamentary soldiers, who had wrested the place from the Royalists and who amused themselves, in their grim fashion, with infinite hacking and hewing in the cathedral.'

HENRY JAMES 1879

THE MARKET CROSS *Chichester, Sussex*

CHICHESTER, THE MARKET CROSS 1890 22618

FISHBOURNE, THE ROMAN PALACE C1968 F132002

Fishbourne in West Sussex is one of the earliest and most luxurious Roman buildings in Britain, and is rightly called a palace. The earliest buildings on the site were timber military granaries. In the AD60s a stone house was built; it had a courtyard, a bath complex and an ornamental garden, and it was probably built for the local British chieftain, Cogidubnus, who was on the best of terms with the Romans. Then in about AD75 the palace was built, incorporating the earlier house. The walls were decorated with marble veneers, stucco friezes, and murals, and there were many beautiful mosaic floors; this one (F132002, above) shows in the centre a winged cupid riding a dolphin, with sea panthers and sea horses in the surrounding semi-circles.

The palace was altered over a long period of time. At the end of the 3rd century a disastrous fire destroyed the palace, and it was not until 1960 that the laying of a water main brought about its discovery. For whatever reason, the skeleton shown in F132008 (opposite, far right) was buried in the ruins of the building some time after its destruction.

The building was magnificent, and would have been comparable to those of Rome itself. The rooms had painted friezes and many mosaics, some of the earliest in Britain. There was a colonnaded courtyard, a reception hall, and a scented garden. The mosaic in F132021(opposite) has a geometric design; it consists of thousands of tessellated fired pottery pieces, of various colours, which were laid into soft mortar. Photograph F132017 (opposite above) shows part of a hypocaust (under-floor heating system) and the remains of mosaic floors.

Top: FISHBOURNE, THE ROMAN PALACE C1968 F132017

Left: FISHBOURNE, THE ROMAN PALACE C1968 F132021

Above: FISHBOURNE, THE ROMAN PALACE C1968 F132008

This present-day fishing village and yachting centre was once a place of much greater importance. The Romans, the Saxons and the Vikings (who stole the church bells) all landed in this area during their invasions, and King Canute had a palace here. Bosham is traditionally the place where King Canute tried to hold back the tide, in an effort to prove to his fawning courtiers that he was not all-powerful as they suggested. The church is said to be the burial place of King Canute's second daughter, who died in infancy.

KING CANUTE

Far left:
BOSHAM, THE CHURCH
AND THE GREEN 1903
50919P

Near left:
BOSHAM, THE CHURCH
1903   50916

Below:
AN ARTIST'S
IMPRESSION OF A
NORMAN SHIP, FROM
THE BAYEUX TAPESTRY
F6019

Bosham features on the Bayeux Tapestry, for in 1064 King Edward the Confessor's brother-in-law Harold Godwinson (later King Harold) sailed from Bosham to Normandy, and set in train the events that led to the Battle of Hastings and his own death. It is not clear whether Harold's visit was accident or design: some accounts say that Edward had sent Harold to see William, but others say that Harold only ended up in Normandy after being shipwrecked. The Bayeux Tapestry shows Harold praying in Bosham church before setting out, and later depicts how, in Nomandy, Harold agreed (or was forced) to swear on holy relics that after King Edward's death he would uphold William's claim to the English throne. This was one of William's main claims to the throne; when Harold broke this vow, William made this one of his justifications for invading England. Because a sacred vow appeared to have been broken, William was also able to call upon the support of the Pope for the Norman Conquest. 1066 is sometimes referred to as 'The Year of Three Kings', for Edward the Confessor, Harold II and William I all wore the crown of England in that year.

CHANCTONBURY RING
Washington, Sussex

On the Sussex Downs, on the scarp above the village of Washington, stands the small hill-fort of Chanctonbury Ring. It is now festooned with beech trees, planted in 1760, which make this spot a landmark visible for miles. The inner compound contains the remains of two Roman buildings, including a temple, proof that this fort too succumbed to the influence of the Romans. In later years this hilltop site was used as an Armada beacon.

Where the past still lives with a peculiar power

Jacquetta Hawkes, in her 'Guide to the Prehistoric and Roman Monuments in England and Wales' (1951), describes Chanctonbury Ring compellingly: 'When as a child I first stepped across the Iron Age rampart among the slender beech-trunks, I felt that I had left the sun for a strange shadowy cage, a world entirely of its own. Although I did not know that the foundations of a Romano-Celtic temple (dedicated probably to some local Celtic divinity) were buried beneath my feet, I was possessed by a most potent sense of natural sanctity; the tree-trunks through which I could see the bright world of the Downs on one side and the swooning distances of the Weald on the other were themselves the pillars of a temple … It still seems to me that Chanctonbury Ring is one of those places where the past lives with some peculiar power.'

THE LONG MAN

Wilmington, Sussex

The design of this huge, ancient giant, on the South Downs near Eastbourne (W406009, left), is cleverly elongated vertically to counteract the effect of foreshortening when viewed from below the hillside. It is one of the largest representations of the human figure in the world at 70m from head to toe. It was 'discovered' in 1873 and restored the following year, but when it was first made is uncertain; it is in an area rich in Neolithic and Bronze Age remains, including the Windover Hill long barrow close by. The two uprights on each side of the Long Man have been interpreted as spears, tools, symbols of high office, or even a doorway. Another theory is that the figure may represent a pilgrim, and this may link it to the medieval Wilmington Priory nearby.

Left: WILMINGTON, THE LONG MAN C1960 W406009

THE DEVIL'S DYKE	Brighton, Sussex

The Devil's Dyke, an Iron Age hill-fort, gives visitors long views from the northern scarp of the Sussex Downs across the Weald. The fort is oval in plan with a well-preserved rampart. The legend is that the Dyke was dug by the Devil, infuriated by the Christian piety of the Sussex people, in the hope that the sea would rush through to flood the Weald and drown them. His plot was foiled by an old woman who rushed up the hill with a lighted candle held behind a sieve, which fooled a cockerel into thinking it was dawn. Hearing the cockerel crow, the Devil abandoned his task and fled, for he cannot bear sunlight.

Above: BRIGHTON, THE DEVIL'S DYKE 1894 33764

THE OLD YEW TREE *Wilmington, Sussex*

How old is this tree? It is now generally recognised by scientists that many yew trees in Britain are 2,000 years old or even older. This beautiful specimen, very large and needing props to support it in this photograph (left), could therefore have stood here as long as the Long Man has, perhaps.

Britain has more ancient yews than most other countries, many of them in churchyards. This is because from ancient times, all over the world, the yew has been associated with death, rebirth and immortality; in many cultures it is the tree of life (a concept which can be traced back to Neolithic times), and associated with the mother goddess, and some traditions link the yew with the tree of knowledge. Celtic, Nordic and Anglo-Saxon myths share this belief in the yew as the tree of death and rebirth, and hence yew trees would have been planted in sacred places, particularly burial places, as the protector of the soul during its transition form death to eternal life. When Christianity came to Britain, it took over the sacred places of the old religion, and indeed the symbolism of the yew fitted very well with the Christian message of resurrection; thus a new Christian church would be built beside the sacred yew. How fitting it is that today yew trees are the source of life-giving anti-cancer drugs.

Left: WILMINGTON, THE OLD YEW TREE C1960
W406006

Above:
PEVENSEY, THE CASTLE
1894 34477

PEVENSEY CASTLE

Pevensey, Sussex

'The Groans of the Britons'

The period of Roman administration of Britain lasted until the early 5th century, when the empire on the Continent came under increasing threat from the barbarians beyond the frontier, especially when the Vandals, Alans and Suevi crossed the frozen Rhine in AD406. The offshore province of Britannia must have seemed relatively unimportant. The last legions were recalled from Britain to help with defence closer to home, and in AD410 the Emperor Honorius famously wrote to the local councils of Britain, the civitates, telling them to undertake their own defence from then on. Never again was the empire secure enough for troops to be freed for action in Britain. 'To Agitius, now Consul for the third time: the groans of the Britons … The barbarians drive us to the sea; the sea throws us back on the barbarians: thus two modes of death await us, we are either slain or drowned.' This, according to Gildas in his 'De Excidio et Conquestu Britanniae' (cAD535), was a letter written by the Britons, appealing for help against attack by the Scots, Picts and North Sea raiders. However, no aid was forthcoming. After the withdrawal of Rome, Britain entered a long period of attack and settlement by Jutes, Angles, Saxons and Scandinavian peoples which lasted until the Norman Conquest of 1066 – the Normans themselves were descended from Norsemen who had settled in northern France.

In the 4th century the Romans built Anderida here, one of their chain of Saxon Shore forts intended to defend the Roman province of Britannia from Saxon raiders. Much later William the Conqueror had a castle built within the Roman walls, both of which survive. In Roman and medieval times the site was beside the sea, but this has now retreated half a mile away. The Anglo-Saxon Chronicle records the arrival of Aelle and his three sons, Cymen, Wlencing and Cissa, in three ships in AD480. They fought several battles against the Britons, and attacked Anderida. The Chronicle records: 'Aelle and Cissa beset the fort of Andredesceaster and slew all that were therein and not one Briton was left alive'.

KING HAROLD'S BATTLE   *Battle, Sussex*

William the Conqueror's claim to the throne, and the Battle of Hastings

William the Conqueror's claim to the throne was very slight indeed. He was a distant cousin of the English King Edward the Confessor, and William's right to the English throne stemmed from Edward's nominating him as his heir in 1051. However, under Anglo-Saxon law this was not a matter for the king alone to decide; Harold Godwinson of Wessex was the choice of the Witan, the council who advised the king. But William's belief in his right to the throne was strengthened when Harold Godwinson swore on holy relics to support William's claim. Was Harold tricked into the oath, with the sacred relics hidden under the table? Was the oath made under duress? Harold did not consider the oath to be binding; when Edward died, the Witan appointed Harold to be king, and he agreed.

A third claimant to the throne was King Harald Hardrada of Norway. He arrived in northern England with an invasion force in September 1066, assisted by Tostig Godwinson, Harold's brother. Harold made a swift forced march north, and defeated the Norwegian forces at the Battle of Stamford Bridge. But Harold's enjoyment of his victory was short-lived, as news was brought to him that William of Normandy had just landed on the Sussex coast near Pevensey on 28 September. Harold and his exhausted, battle-weary forces marched the 250 miles from Yorkshire in nine days, and met the Norman army at what history now calls the Battle of Hastings on 14 October 1066. After a long struggle, King Harold was killed; the defeated remnants of the Anglo-Saxon forces fled, and King William had won the day.

The town that has grown up at the gates of the abbey that William the Conqueror founded to mark his victory at the Battle of Hastings in 1066 is known simply as Battle. This alone says more than any words could do about the importance of that battle in the development of the English nation.

The high altar of Battle Abbey was later built on the spot where Harold fell at the Battle of Hastings. This stone tablet (left) in the grounds of Battle Abbey still marks the site where Anglo-Saxon England ended and Norman Britain began.

Opposite: BATTLE, THE ABBEY GATEWAY 1890 25386

Above: BATTLE, THE TABLET ERECTED TO KING HAROLD 1910 62974

QUEEN ELIZABETH'S WELL

Winchelsea, Sussex

WINCHELSEA, QUEEN ELIZABETH'S WELL 1906 53486

To reach this well the visitor must negotiate a narrow path which leads to Spring Steps (to the left in 53486). The well is one of those from which the inhabitants of Winchelsea used to draw their water – the other wells were Pipe Well, Friars Well, New Well, and Vale or St Leonard's Well. It is said that those who drink the water from one of these wells will never leave Winchelsea – wherever they go, their hearts will still be here. This well was always known as St Katherine's Well until the visit of Elizabeth I to Winchelsea in 1573. The cult of St Katherine (or Catherine) of Alexandria, who was tortured by razor-sharp wheels, was a popular one in medieval England, when she was held up as a model of piety to young women.

THE ROMAN ROAD — *Tenterden, Kent*

During the Roman occupation, the main route for the Roman forces was Watling Street, which went along the Thames Estuary to Londinium. However, the Romans did penetrate the forest areas of Kent, which they called Anderida, mainly by improving the existing iron workers' trackways. There is evidence of a Roman road from Benenden to Ashford and thence to Canterbury, which went through the area north of what became Tenterden – sections of this road can still be walked today.

Ebbsfleet in Pegwell Bay is traditionally believed to be the spot where Hengist and Horsa landed in the 5th century, signalling the beginning of the Anglo-Saxon, Jutish and Danish occupation of Britain. Pegwell Bay now houses the replica Viking dragon-headed longship which was rowed and sailed from Denmark to Broadstairs in Kent in 1949 to celebrate the 1,500th anniversary of this event, although the term 'Viking' was a little inaccurate for the 5th century.

Above: TENTERDEN, THE ROMAN ROAD FROM BROWN'S CORNER 2004 T24701K

THE VIKING SHIP — *Pegwell, Kent*

PEGWELL, THE DANISH VIKING SHIP 'HUGIN' C1955 P20023

Anglo-Saxon Settlement

The term Anglo-Saxon refers to settlers from the Germanic regions of Europe such as Saxony and Angeln, who came to Britain after the fall of the Roman Empire around AD410. Although settlers also came from Jutland and Frisia, the term has now come to be used for all these peoples. These new settlers were mainly farmers, and most English villages developed from Anglo-Saxon settlements. The four main Anglo-Saxon kingdoms were Northumbria, Mercia, East Anglia and Wessex, and in later years the country as a whole became known as Angleland (England). Many of our words came from their language, including the days of the week: Woden's day for Wednesday, Thor's day for Thursday, for instance, after their gods. The Anglo-Saxon people were originally pagan, but the arrival of St Augustine in AD597 saw the beginnings of missions to convert the English to Christianity.

The Pharos, or Roman lighthouse, is a weatherworn shell whose top storey was rebuilt in the 15th century. The Romans erected it as a beacon for their galleys sailing over from Gaul – Roman Dover (Dubris) was a base of the Classis Britannica, the fleet of the Roman navy operating in Britain. The Pharos is octagonal in plan, and the design is similar to the Pharos of Alexandria. Adjoining it is St Martin's in the Castle, one of the most important pre-Conquest buildings surviving in this country, although much restored in 1862 and 1888 – its builders re-used Roman materials. It became the Garrison Church in 1267, a position it still retains today.

Above: DOVER, ST MARTIN'S IN THE CASTLE
CHURCH AND THE PHAROS C1874 7081
Right: DOVER, THE PHAROS C1965 D50103

HISTORIC CANTERBURY

Canterbury, Kent

In AD597 Pope Gregory became concerned about the spiritual wellbeing of those souls who lived in what he still thought of as the Roman province of Britannia. Gregory called on Augustine, a monk from his own monastery, to travel to 'Durovernum Cantiacorum' (soon to become Cantwaraburh) with a group of fellow Christians to establish the word of God there and build a church. At first Augustine was against the idea because he was afraid of the hostility he would meet from the Saxons when he reached the shores of Kent. But after listening to Pope Gregory's words of encouragement, Augustine and his fellow monks set sail, and on their arrival were welcomed by the King of Kent, Ethelbert, and his wife Queen Bertha. Frankish-born Bertha was already a practising Christian, and her husband had presented her with St Martin's Church (as chronicled by Bede). This church, possibly the oldest in Britain, has a chancel which has Roman features. It was named after St Martin, the patron saint of Tours, the French town in which Bertha had grown up.

Pillars of tiles were used to support the floors of the Roman bathhouse in Canterbury, so that warm air could circulate as part of the Roman hypocaust system of under-floor central heating (C18702k, left). Today these are on show on the ground floor of Waterstone's bookshop in St Margaret's Street.

Above:
CANTERBURY,
ST MARTIN'S
CHURCH, QUEEN
BERTHA'S TOMB
1898 40851

Right: DRAWING
OF ST MARTIN'S
CHURCH,
CANTERBURY

Left:
CANTERBURY,
THE ROMAN BATHS,
ST MARGARET'S
STREET 2005
C18702K

KIT'S COTY HOUSE

Aylesford, Kent

Above: AYLESFORD, KIT'S COTY HOUSE 1898 41555

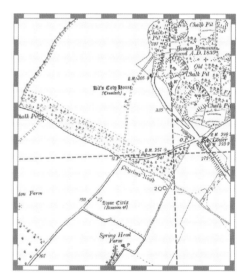

To the west of the A229 is Kent's most famous Neolithic burial chamber. The capstone, supported by three large uprights, measures 13ft by 9ft, and the earthen mound which originally covered the stones was 170ft long. At the west end there used to be a large stone known as the General's Tombstone, but this was blown up in 1867 because it hampered farming; it was probably the last remnant of a ring of stones round the mound. Legend has it that the burial mound was the tomb of Catigern, a British chief killed fighting against the Saxons, although it is actually far older than this event - it dates from about 5,000 years ago. It is said that this ancient monument takes its name from a local shepherd named Kit who used these stones as a shelter in the 17th century ('coty' means 'small house' in the local dialect), although there is another theory that the name derives from the Celtic 'ked koit', 'the tomb in the wood'.

THE COUNTLESS STONES   *Aylesford, Kent*

AYLESFORD, THE COUNTLESS STONES C1960 A85044

There is a legend that it is impossible to count the number of stones correctly, hence the name. The site consists of a group of 21 large and small stones, which are probably the jumbled remains of the chamber of a long barrow. It is reported that a farmer knocked down the stones in 1690. In the 1930s, traces of the mound covering these stones could still be seen. The trees seen in this photograph have now been removed. In the 17th century William Stukeley published a reconstruction of these stones, which were formed into a D-shaped structure. There are several folklore associations with the Countless Stones. At one time it was believed that if young women lay on the stones overnight, they would be able to conceive. Another tale tells the story of an Aylesford baker who was on his way home one winter's night when he saw the devil sitting on the stones. The devil challenged the baker to count the stones and tell him the correct number – if he got it right, the devil would grant the baker great wealth, but if he got it wrong, the devil would claim his soul. The baker counted the stones correctly by placing a loaf of bread on each stone as he counted it, to make sure that he did not count a stone twice. He won his bet and saved his soul.

RECULVER TOWERS
Herne Bay, Kent

CAESAR'S WELL

Keston, Greater London

Legend has it that Caesar's Well was found by Roman soldiers when they went looking for water in the area. They saw a raven drinking near their camp, and on investigating found a copious spring. This is the source of the River Ravensbourne, which eventually discharges into the Thames via Deptford Creek. The ravens in Bromley's coat of arms represent the Ravensbourne.

Above: KESTON, CAESAR'S WELL C1960 K152024

Left: HERNE BAY, RECULVER, THE TOWERS C1955 R14033

These twin towers are all that remain of a Saxon and medieval church, part of which was blown up in 1809 to prevent it from falling into the sea. The church stands within the walls of a Roman fort called Regulbium. An old local legend said that on stormy nights the sound of crying babies could be heard here; some basis for this story was found when archaeologists excavating the fort found a number of baby skeletons. Whether these were buried as some form of sacrifice or were exposed as unwanted children, or were placed there for some other reason, will now never be known.

SILBURY HILL
Avebury, Wiltshire

Silbury Hill, near Avebury and Marlborough, is the largest man-made mound in Europe, about 40m high with a diameter of 165m and a flat top 30m across. It was once thought (justifiably at that time) to be a large burial mound for an important Bronze Age chieftain. Excavations, however, have revealed no human remains; one thing they did discover was that the building of the mound was started in August – in the foundations was evidence of flying ants! It is about 4,500 years old. Apart from its core and foundation layers of gravel, clay and soil, it is made entirely of chalk, excavated from the surrounding ditch. It predates the Roman road, now the A4, whose early track can be seen in the photograph. In 1883 Silbury Hill became the first site in Britain to be classified as an ancient monument. The purpose of Silbury Hill still remains a mystery.

Above: AVEBURY, SILBURY HILL 1902 48647

The Legend of Silbury Hill

An old legend tells a different story about Silbury Hill. The townsfolk of Marlborough and Devizes were always at loggerheads. Marlborough, coming off the worst at one fight, sought revenge by using the services of the Devil, who offered to wipe out Devizes by dropping a hill on the town. This threat was heard by St John, who in due course warned Devizes. Their townsfolk sent their biggest liar, who was the oldest inhabitant, to put the Devil off. With a sack filled with old clothes and shoes, he met the Devil near Beckhampton, and there asked him the time. Old Nick was tired of carrying the hill, and asked in his turn how far to Devizes. The old man said that he would never get there that night or for some time to come, as he had left Devizes as a young man and during his long journey he had worn out the clothes and boots he was carrying. Dumping these on the ground, he enlarged his tale. Old Nick was incredulous, but the old man stuck to his story, and fooled the Devil into believing it. Flinging the hill down from his shoulders, the Devil departed in a flash of lightning. Devizes is still there, and the hill at Silbury stands for all to see, so the tale must be true!

AVEBURY

Avebury, Wiltshire

Avebury is the largest and most impressive henge monument in Britain. It was completed by about 2,600BC, at a time when Stonehenge consisted only of a bank and ditch. Avebury's massive bank and inner ditch (the circumference is about 1.3 kilometres) encloses a circle of 98 sarsen stones, and within them were two smaller circles and a further setting of stones near the centre. Unlike Stonehenge, the stones at Avebury are unworked, but they were chosen for their size and shape – taller, narrower stones tend to alternate with shorter, broader ones. Sarsen stones (the word sarsen derives from Saracen, and means foreign or strange) can be found on the Marlborough Downs about two miles away. There were four entrances into the hedge marked by larger stones; these entrances are now used by modern roads, and some village houses stand within the monument. Modern village life and ancient stones live side by side in a common and mutual existence where the past is indelibly a living part of the present. Alexander Keiller (of marmalade fame) bought the site in 1934 to save it for the nation, and serious archaeological work began. The Avebury we see today owes its existence to these excavations. In an experiment it took Keiller four days and twelve men to raise one stone using the Neolithic method of levers, timbers and manpower. During the 1940s Avebury was handed over to the National Trust, and it is now a World Heritage Site. Recent archaeological investigations have revealed an arc of at least 15 more stones buried in the Avebury stone circle itself. Although there are no immediate plans to raise the stones, it may well be possible to create a 3-D computer image of the stones using ground-probing radar, and thus 'raise' them virtually.

Top: AVEBURY CIRCLE C1955 A80001   *Above:* AVEBURY, THE COVE 1899 44860

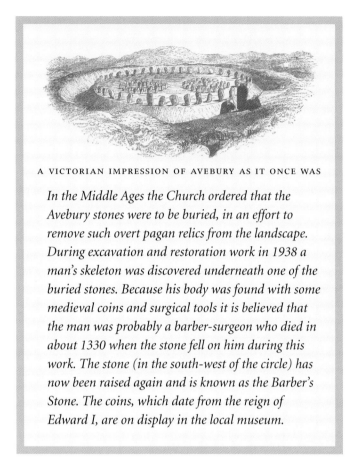

In the Middle Ages the Church ordered that the Avebury stones were to be buried, in an effort to remove such overt pagan relics from the landscape. During excavation and restoration work in 1938 a man's skeleton was discovered underneath one of the buried stones. Because his body was found with some medieval coins and surgical tools it is believed that the man was probably a barber-surgeon who died in about 1330 when the stone fell on him during this work. The stone (in the south-west of the circle) has now been raised again and is known as the Barber's Stone. The coins, which date from the reign of Edward I, are on display in the local museum.

These stones form part of the West Kennet Avenue, a ceremonial avenue that links the south-eastern entrance of Avebury to a smaller stone circle, the Sanctuary, about one mile away (the Avenue was partly reconstructed in the 1930s). Along this sacred avenue it is probable that dead bodies were carried from the Sanctuary to the temple of Avebury. Excavations have discovered burials beside some of the stones. Neolithic people were the first to settle and farm, rather than following a nomadic existence; thus their ritual sites often seem to be linked to the agricultural cycle and fertility rites, and it has been suggested that the shape of the Avenue stones – alternating pillar and lozenge shapes – represented male and female fertility. There was once a similar avenue, the Beckhampton Avenue, to the south-west, but little of this remains.

In the middle of the northern inner circle (of which little survives) stood the Cove (44860, previous page); it originally consisted of three or four stones, of which two now remain. It is possible that bodies were left here on funerary platforms to decompose, before a skeletal burial was carried out in one of the many long barrows that surround Avebury. The barn and outbuilding seen in this photograph were demolished in the 1940s as part of the long-overdue restoration programme. One of these stones weighs 100 metric tonnes, the equivalent of two Chieftain tanks, heavier than any stone at Stonehenge.

Above: AVEBURY, THE AVENUE C1955 A80023

Opposite top: AVEBURY, EXCAVATIONS C1908 A80501

This remarkable photograph was taken during the excavations at Avebury carried out by Harold St George Gray, who had been engaged by the British Association for the Advancement of Science to investigate the age of stone circles. Gray had worked as assistant to General Pitt-Rivers, the father of modern archaeology, and had learnt from him the importance of systematic recording and proper preservation of finds. He dug at Avebury in 1908, 1909, 1911 and 1914, and again in 1922, and here we are probably looking at his first excavations of the bank and ditch on the southern side of the circle. The modern stone circle expert Aubrey Burl could have been looking at this photograph when he wrote: '[Gray's] cloth-capped labourers, collarless but wearing their habitual waistcoats, without any mechanical assistance picked and shovelled an average of six hundred tons of chalk from each trench, heaving the rubble up ladders as their cuttings sank down through the silt into the darkening shadows of the chalk' ('Prehistoric Avebury', 1979). Gray showed that the ditch had originally been about 10m deep, and his finds of human and animal bones, pottery, and flint and antler tools enabled him to date the building of the monument accurately to the very late Neolithic era.

Hardy's Devil's Den

Thomas Hardy (1840–1928) set his short story 'What the Shepherd Saw' at the Devil's Den (or the Devil's Door, as he called it): 'To the south, in the direction of the young shepherd's idle gaze, there rose one conspicuous object above the uniform moonlit plateau, and only one. It was a Druidical trilithon, consisting of three oblong stones in the form of a doorway, two on end, and one across as a lintel. Each stone had been worn, scratched, washed, nibbled, split, and otherwise attacked by ten thousand different weathers; but now the blocks looked shapely and little the worse for wear, so beautifully were they silvered over by the light of the moon.'

Devil's Den, near Marlborough in Wiltshire, is an example of how the plough has destroyed a fine ancient monument. This was once a magnificent Neolithic chambered long barrow that was covered with an earthen mound, probably originally about 230ft long; when it was first constructed, the barrow would have shone brilliant white, thanks to the chalky soil. Drawings by Stukeley, the 18th-century antiquarian, show a chamber flanked by a façade of sarsen stones; by the 20th century the barrow was largely destroyed, and two of the stones and a capstone were re-erected and partly concreted in place in 1921. A local legend tells that a rabbit with fiery coals for eyes sits on the capstone at midnight and watches the devil try to pull it down with eight white oxen.

Right: FYFIELD, THE DEVIL'S DEN
1901 47674

THE DEVIL'S DEN *Fyfield, Wiltshire*

THE WHITE HORSE   *Westbury, Wiltshire*

Above: WESTBURY, THE WHITE HORSE AND BRATTON CAMP C1900   45365

The Westbury White Horse, standing out prominently overlooking the Avon valley, was re-cut in 1778 to a design nearer to its present day appearance. The process was overseen by a Mr George Gee, who shouted instructions through a megaphone from a mile away. He apparently felt that the older version was not a sufficiently good representation of a horse. There is evidence to suggest that the original design would have more closely resembled the Uffington White Horse (see page 138), although its origins are not known. Immediately above it is Bratton Camp, an Iron Age hill-fort. Its double bank and ditch enclose an area of about 10 hectares, and inside is a Neolithic long barrow – excavations found two adult burials.

The white horses of the chalk downland in southern England are among the best-known features of the countryside. Other large-scale hillside figures cut into the turf (including giants, birds, crosses, badges and others) can be found all over Britain. This form of turf cutting is a very old and widespread art, albeit a rather obscure one, but it does seem to be a peculiarly English practice.

ANCIENT CROSS

Ramsbury, Wiltshire

Several fragments of carved Saxon stonework were found in the wall of Holy Cross Church at Ramsbury during restoration work in 1891. These include sections of two Saxon crosses and some tomb covers, which are now on display in the church.

Left: RAMSBURY, THE ANCIENT CROSS IN THE CHURCH OF THE HOLY CROSS C1955 R6020

STONEHENGE 1887 19800

Stonehenge, the most famous stone circle in the world, was built and adapted in three phases, over a huge time span (about 15 centuries) between approximately 2,950BC and 1,600BC. The first Stonehenge was a circular bank and ditch, probably containing timber uprights. It was during the second phase (approx 2,900–2,400BC) that new timber settings were erected in the north-east entrance and at the centre. During these early phases, it seems that the purpose of the monument was the observation of the movements of the moon through the entrance. It may also have been linked with death and funerary rituals – deposits of burnt human bone dating from this period have been found. In the third phase (2,550–1,600BC) the Stonehenge we see today was developed. The Hele Stone (and another stone west of it) was erected outside the monument marking the point where the midsummer sun rose. Bluestone pillars were erected – they had been brought all the way from the Preseli mountains in Wales – surrounding the Altar Stone. Then came a horseshoe-shaped setting of five large trilithons. Around this were more bluestones, then a ring of sarsen stones. The Avenue was constructed, emphasising the change of observation from the moon to the sun. But Stonehenge was not just a temple; it was a place where people met to engage in all kinds of ceremonies, so around it are many related monuments, including a cursus and many barrows.

Despite its colourful name, the Slaughter Stone (seen in 80939, previous page) was probably originally part of a gateway, and is unlikely to have been used for ritual sacrifices.

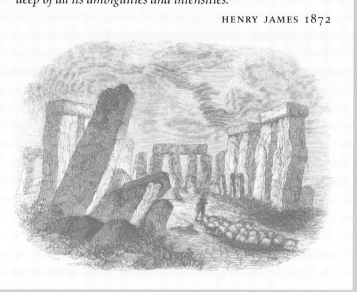

Stonehenge — a hackneyed shrine?

'Stonehenge is a rather hackneyed shrine of pilgrimage. At the time of my former visit a picnic party was making libations of beer on the dreadful altar-sites. But the mighty mystery of the place has not yet been stared out of countenance; and as on this occasion there were no picnickers we were left to drink deep of all its ambiguities and intensities.'

HENRY JAMES 1872

The view we see above (80950) is possibly one of the most photographed. It shows the Hele stone between the middle uprights. The monument is perennially popular with modern-day Druids who congregate here to celebrate the summer solstice, when the sun is said to rise directly above the Hele stone on the longest day of the year, 21 June. However, the sun does not actually rise directly above it, and never did, even 4,000 years ago. Recent research suggests that at some stage rituals marking the winter solstice became important, and Stonehenge may have been used for ceremonies to call back the sun at the darkest time of the year. Beyond the Hele stone, 40 posts mark the axis of moonrise at the winter solstice, the shortest day of the year. Somehow, even all that time ago, the ancient stargazers had realised that the moon's position on the shortest day changes from year to year, over a lunar cycle of 18.61 years, and these posts marked all the positions. Four stones on the outer circle of the enclosure, known as Station Stones, also marked the intersection of lunar sight-lines.

Above left: STONEHENGE, THE HELE STONE 1928   80950
Below: STONEHENGE 1887   19797T

As we look southwards from the Hele stone (19796, above) through the middle arch, we can see the tallest stone of the inner horseshoe of trilithons. The oldest tenon joint in Britain can be seen, laboriously hammered out with football-shaped flint hammers. The lintel that capped this stone contained the mortise to hold it in place.

All must surrender to their power

'We may feel that publicity has destroyed the spirit of this too-famous building; yet once among the stones all but the most stubbornly resistant moods must surrender to their power. The massive, roughly squared blocks of sarsen seem to possess a forceful presence which asserts itself within the human consciousness. Their silvery grey colour fills the eye but now shows itself to be variegated with dark lichens and with the shadow of grotesque fissures and hollows worn by centuries of rain and frost … The uprights with their heavy lintels have stood for thousands of years and seem eternal'.

JACQUETTA HAWKES,
'A GUIDE TO THE PREHISTORIC AND ROMAN MONUMENTS
IN ENGLAND AND WALES' (1951)

Top: STONEHENGE 1887 19796

Above: STONEHENGE C1960 S205108

STONEHENGE, THE HELE STONE OR THE FRIAR'S HEEL
1928 80952

Sometimes known as the Heel Stone, legend says that this stone was a boulder that the Devil threw at a monk or friar, which pinned him to the ground by his heel. 'Hele' is probably a more accurate name, since it reflects the link with sun rituals that probably occurred at Stonehenge (from the Greek 'helios', meaning 'sun'). The 12th-century historian and storyteller Geoffrey of Monmouth, who popularised the tales of King Arthur and Merlin in his 'History of the Kings of Britain', called Stonehenge the Giant's Dance, and said that it was moved from Ireland to Wiltshire by the wizard Merlin.

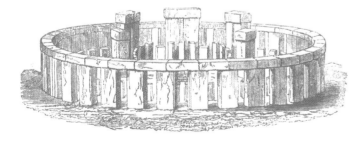

A VICTORIAN IMPRESSION OF STONEHENGE
IN ITS COMPLETE STATE

OLD SARUM

Salisbury, Wiltshire

OLD SARUM, THE OLD ROMAN ROAD (THE PORTWAY) C1965 O58021

Old Sarum began its life as an Iron Age hill-fort built around 500BC. Not only are the huge bank and ditches of the hill-fort still intact, but the original zigzag entrance on the east is still the only way into the 56-acre green enclosure. This hilltop was chosen because several ancient downland tracks were close by. The Langford Way and others came from the north-west and north off the famous east-west Harrow Way, which ran along the line of the present A303 near Stonehenge; another route, today called the South Hants Ridgeway, came from the east over Pepperbox; and others came up from the coast and south-west, such as the Salisbury Way from Cranborne Chase. This last route, later called Racecourse Way or Shaftesbury Drove, remained a road until the 1750s. The site became known as Old Sarum after the town of New Sarum, or Salisbury, was developed away from this windy hilltop in the 13th century, around the new cathedral of St Mary.

Above left: OLD SARUM C1955 O58168

Below left: OLD SARUM, FROM THE SOUTH 1913 65294

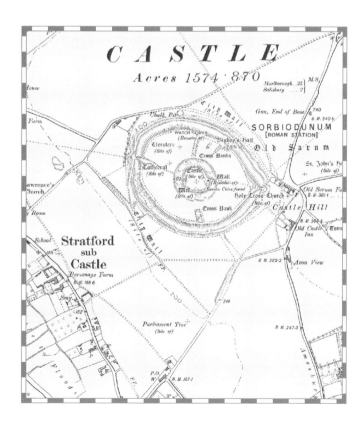

When the Romans invaded southern England they captured the hilltop settlement of Old Sarum, and soon exploited the advantages of the site for a garrison signal station and communications centre, which they called Sorbiodunum. Four Roman roads centre on the hill, leading away north-east (past the present-day RAF Boscombe Down) to Cunetio (Mildenhall) near Marlborough, westwards across the Avon valley through Grovely Forest to the Mendip lead mines, past Stratford-sub-Castle and away to Dorchester to the south-west, and going eastwards along the Portway to Winchester. Their routes can still be clearly seen and traced; there is a Roman road in Bemerton, and the Portway (O58021, page 121), which passes Old Sarum Airfield, is still so named today.

Saxon invasions in the 5th and 6th centuries led to the eventual capture of the hilltop village in around AD557, and the new settlers soon named it Searoburgh, sometimes translated as 'the town on the dry hill'. Over the next five centuries the spelling slowly changed to Sarisberie, and the Saxon village grew in importance, becoming a mint and a centre of local administration. The small village of Wilton, down in the nearby Wylye valley, was one of King Alfred's 'capitals' - and gives its name to the county of Wiltshire (Wiltonshire) – but it was Sarisberie (Old Sarum) which offered greater protection for the local population, since Wilton was twice destroyed by Danish raids.

Left:
OLD SARUM, THE EXCAVATIONS 1913
65302

By the time of the Norman Conquest the village at Old Sarum was important enough to be the place where William the Conqueror arranged for the building, in the middle of the old fort, of an impressive new Norman stone castle with its own walls and a deep ditch and bank. Close by, below the castle on the north-west inside the prehistoric ramparts, a beautiful Norman cathedral was built between 1078 and 1092 by order of Bishop Osmund, who was also the king's chancellor. The town of Salisbury on its windy hilltop was now important enough to have its own Norman bishopric. Osmund not only introduced the system of collegiate organisation later used by many bishoprics and 'the Sarum use' as an order of service, but also carried out many miracles of healing. Osmund died in 1099; his remains were later reburied in the new cathedral that we see in Salisbury today, and he was finally canonised in 1457.

In photograph 65295 (below left) we see a wooden hut on the site of the dig, possibly offering temporary storage for excavated objects. Here archaeologists would come to check the progress of the excavation and to inspect the finds as they came to light. Photograph 65303 (opposite) shows the display of artefacts at Old Sarum, doubtless intended to give information to archaeologists, not for use as a postcard, as Frith photographs usually were. The lack of information labels suggests that the display was intended for viewing by professionals only. There is a single sign – 'Please do not touch'. Half-obscured, it is unlikely it would have been obeyed by excited archaeologists. The artefacts shown here are from the excavation of the cathedral and inner bailey carried out between 1909 and 1915 by the Society of Antiquaries under Sir William St John Hope. One notable find was a quantity of very rare pieces of verde-antico and red porphyry. It is likely that the items on the second shelf down show the sherds reconstructed into jugs and pots. Other items on the shelves include iron keys, some fragments of Norman stonework, and animal bones.

Above left: OLD SARUM C1955 O58173

Below left: OLD SARUM, THE KITCHEN 1913 65295

Opposite: OLD SARUM, OBJECTS DISCOVERED DURING EXCAVATIONS 1913 65303

THE SAXON CHURCH

Bradford-on-Avon, Wiltshire

This Saxon church had been concealed by sheds and buildings for many centuries. It was rediscovered in the 19th century by Canon W H R Jones, a keen antiquarian; he came across references to it in a text dated 1125. Excavations outside revealed the walls, and repairs revealed the carvings. It is believed that the lower part of the walls belongs to the church erected by St Aldhelm as long ago as cAD700. The simplicity and to some extent the austerity of St Laurence's contrasts with the richness of the churches of later times; we are not used to churches without stained glass, or in fact without windows at all. This church would have been lit by candles.

Arthur Mee in his 'King's England' series says about the church: 'It is naked and bare, and all the better for that'. The chancel arch is the narrowest in England at 3ft 6 inches wide. The walls are 2ft 5 inches thick, and the decorations were all cut by Saxon masons. John Chandler and Derek Parker describe the effect of the church on the visitor in 'Wiltshire Churches, an Illustrated History': 'There is an aura of intense mystery, and to submit to its darkness by entering on a sunny day can be a profoundly awesome experience.'

Left: BRADFORD-ON-AVON, ST LAURENCE'S SAXON CHURCH 1900 45383
Above: BRADFORD-ON-AVON, ST LAURENCE'S SAXON CHURCH 1900 45382

ROMAN CASTLE COMBE   *Castle Combe, Wiltshire*

CASTLE COMBE, THE VILLAGE 1904 51507P

The village of Castle Combe was originally the site of a Roman villa; the Normans built a castle here, and for centuries the village was a centre for cloth weaving. Although this one-sided bridge is very old, it is unlikely to actually be of Roman construction; properly named Smart's Bridge, it became known as the Roman bridge because local legend has it that the ghost of a Roman centurion has been seen here standing guard.

Left: CASTLE COMBE, THE OLD ROMAN BRIDGE C1955 C43023

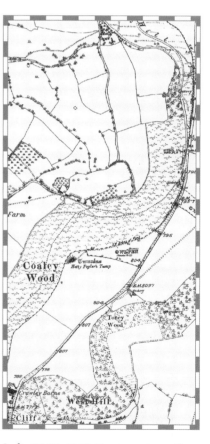

This 180ft-long Neolithic chambered burial mound a mile to the north of Uley is generally known as Hetty Pegler's Tump. It is named after Hester, the wife of Henry Pegler, the local landowner in the 17th century; tump is a Cotswold word for a small hill or mound. It dates from around 3000BC, and is unusual in that its mound is still intact, and visitors can go inside its stone-lined gallery, which is some 20ft long, with two side chambers leading off on the south side. A matching pair on the north side has long since collapsed. When the tomb was first excavated in 1821, at least 15 disarticulated skeletons were found, and about nine more in 1854.

THE TUMULUS *Uley, Gloucestershire*

Left: ULEY, THE TUMULUS C1960 U3008

THE SEVEN SPRINGS

Bisley, Gloucestershire

In a lane off the main village street, seven springs emerge from the hillside below the church and spout a plentiful supply of water. These must have been used by the locals for as long as people have lived in the area, but the structure we see in the photograph was erected in 1863. Water flows from five Gothic arches onto a stone shelf and then into a pool, while two springs at the ends of the semi-circular wall flow into stone troughs. The inscription above the springs reads 'Bless Ye the Lord, Praise Him, And Magnify Him'. Dressing and blessing the wells on Ascension Day is a colourful village affair: after a church service, the villagers process through the streets with the schoolchildren carrying garlands, and the wells are blessed and decorated with spring flowers.

THE HARE MOSAIC   *Cirencester, Gloucestershire*

CIRENCESTER, THE HARE MOSAIC, CORINIUM MUSEUM 2004 C106703K

The mosaic pavements which have been excavated from what must have been the grander houses of Roman Cirencester epitomise the opulence of the households and the artistry of the mosaicist during the Roman period. Classical and mythical, symbolic and symmetrical, these rediscovered mosaic designs and motifs – intricately composed over a millennium and a half ago and since buried under gardens, roadways and buildings – must have been stunning in their own time. Some 80 mosaic pavements have been recorded, some dating from as early as the 2nd century. Outstanding among the rescued and re-laid pavements is one depicting hunting dogs and the seasons, discovered in Dyer Street in 1849, and this hare mosaic, excavated from Beeches Road. The hare, nibbling at a bunch of grapes, is a typical Mediterranean design, but is the only one of its kind found in England. It has become both the logo for the Corinium Museum and an important town symbol.

Above: BIBURY, THE SAXON STONE IN THE NORTH SIDE OF THE CHURCH WALL C1960 B530010

130

THE SAXON CHURCH — *Bibury, Gloucestershire*

At first glance Bibury's church, with its castellated roofline and square tower, looks largely 15th-century. On closer examination, however, its earlier Saxon origins become evident. Set into the exterior of the north, or 'Devil's side', of the building is the carved Saxon motif of interlocking rings shown on page 130, probably part of a cross, a reminder that the town was once part of the ancient Anglo-Saxon kingdom of Mercia. It is believed that there was a church in Bibury by AD750; Saxon grave slabs found here are now in the British Museum.

Above: BIBURY, THE CHURCH C1960 B530019   *Right:* BIBURY, THE CHURCH C1955   B530009

SAXON DEERHURST   *Deerhurst, Gloucestershire*

Odda's chapel

Lying 200 yards south-west of St Mary's, the chapel is a small and simple structure consisting of a nave and chancel built by Earl Odda and dedicated to the Holy Trinity in 1056 (see 47309, above). An inscription records that the chapel is a memorial to Odda's brother Aelfric. The half-timbered building is known as Abbots Court.

Above left: DEERHURST, THE SAXON CHAPEL 1901   47309

Below left: DEERHURST, THE SAXON CHURCH 1901   47306

St Mary's at Deerhurst is one of the finest Saxon churches in Britain, second only in size to Brixworth church in Northamptonshire (see 47306, right). The minster of Deerhurst-on-Severn is known to have existed in the early 9th century, and parts of the church may date from that time. After Danish raids the church was rebuilt cAD930, and the nave of the present building is the oldest part still standing. The west porch was originally built with two storeys; a third floor was added later, with a triangular-headed window looking down into the nave. The aisles were added around 1200.

ROMAN AND SAXON GLOUCESTER

Gloucester, Gloucestershire

GLOUCESTER, ST OSWALD'S PIORY 1923 73681

Gloucester stands on a Roman site. Here alongside the Severn the Romans built a colonia (in other words, an important town whose inhabitants were Roman citizens) – Colonia Nervia Glevensium. The reason for building here was that the site was the first point on the River Severn where a bridge could easily be built. Very little of Roman Gloucester remains. Later, King Aethelred of Mercia laid the foundations of a monastery here in AD681. Periods of instability followed, with Welsh invasions razing the city; fires caused damage too, and the civil war between Beornwulf (King of Mercia) and Coelwulf, his successor, tore the fabric out of the area and destroyed the foundations laid down by the Romans 600 years before. Thereafter the Danes encamped about the city and plundered everything in their wake. But Alfred the Great moved them on after the Battle of Ethandune in AD878, after which he passed the city to his daughter, Aethelflaed, and her husband Aethelred. St Oswald's Priory dates from AD900; it was founded by Aethelflaed to be the home for the remains of St Oswald. The priory is located in the area now known as Kingsholm.

133

COLWALL, THE HEREFORDSHIRE BEACON, THE BRITISH CAMP C1955 C216007

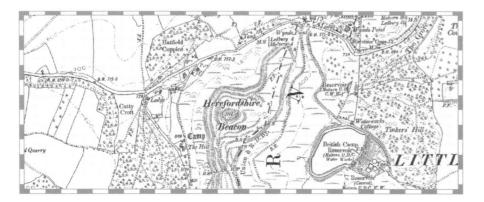

The British camp is an Iron Age hill fort, superbly positioned on the Malvern hills with views in all directions. It is also known as the Herefordshire Beacon, 340m high (1,114ft). It appears to have been constructed over a long period, starting with a small enclosure at the centre of the site. In the late Iron Age the fort was expanded to enclose an area of about 13 hectares; inside there are hut platforms. (A small bank and ditch fortification was constructed in the centre in the 12th century).

The local British tribe, the Dobunni, probably left the camp when the Romans arrived; the popular 19th-century legend that this was the place where Caractacus made his last stand is now discredited. Nevertheless, Sir Edward Elgar used the legend as the basis for a great musical work which he composed with this most evocative hill in mind.

134

THE ROCK CAVES *Stourport-on-Severn, Hereford & Worcester*

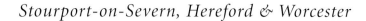

Stourport stands where the River Stour meets the River Severn; it grew in importance after James Brindley built a canal junction there in the 1760s. The meeting of all these waterways proved important in the industrial development of the region. The soft rock cliffs at Redstone Rock above the Severn south of Stourport led to the creation of many caves. Some people believe that these are rock shelters carved out in prehistoric times. There are many legends of witches living in the caves, which indicate that they may well have been pagan sacred sites, and some of the caves were used by hermits in medieval times. Some of these were enlarged and used as dwellings until quite recently. They are now the haunt of visitors strolling out from the nearby towns.

Left: STOURPORT-ON-SEVERN, ROCK CAVES 1931 84630

Below: STOURPORT-ON-SEVERN, REDSTONE CAVES 1931 84629

THE ROMAN BATH HOUSE

Wroxeter, Shropshire

Wroxeter, known in Roman times as Viroconium, was the fourth largest town in Roman Britain and the tribal capital of the Cornovii – it is located near the Wrekin, an Iron Age hill-fort. Today little remains above ground level, but excavations found a legionary fortress (occupied by the Fourteenth Legion and later the Twentieth Legion); however, around AD88 the army moved to Chester, and Wroxeter became a civilian town. The excavations also found a forum (an inscription dates it to AD130), public baths, shops – selling pottery, kitchen wares, and whetstones, among other things - and evidence of post-Roman occupation. This photograph shows the hypocaust heating system for the baths in the foreground, and, behind it, the 'Old Work' – the tallest stretch of Roman masonry surviving anywhere in the country. This was the south wall of the palaestra, or exercise hall, which opened into the baths.

The Wrekin is a large hill in the centre of Shropshire, dominating both Shrewsbury and Telford. The Needle's Eye is the name given to the split in the rock shown here – it is said to have been formed when two giants had a fight. The story first appeared in 'Shropshire Folk-Lore: A Sheaf of Gleanings' by C S Burne and G F Jackson, London 1883:

'Long, long ago, when there were giants in the land, two of them were turned out by the rest, and forced to go and live by themselves, so they set to work to build themselves a hill to live in. In a very short time they had dug out the earth from the bed of the Severn, which runs in the trench they made to the present time, and with it they piled up the Wrekin, intending to make it their home. Those bare patches on the turf between the Bladderstone and the top of the hill, are the marks of their feet, where from that day to this the grass has never grown. But they had not been there long before they quarrelled, and one of them struck at the other with his spade, but failed to hit him, and the spade descending to the ground cleft the solid rock and left the 'Needle's Eye'. Then they began to fight and the giant with the spade (for they seem to have had only one between them – perhaps that was what they quarrelled about!) was getting the best of it at first, but a Raven flew up and pecked at his eyes, and the pain made him shed such a mighty tear that it hollowed out the little basin in the rock which we call the Raven's Bowl, or sometimes the Cuckoo's Cup, which has never been dry since, but is always full of water even in the hottest summer. And now you suppose that it was very easy for the other giant to master the one who had the spade, and when he had done so he determined to put him where he could never trouble anyone again. So he very quickly built up the Ercall Hill beside the Wrekin, and imprisoned his fallen foe within it. There the poor blind giant remains to this day, and in the dead of night you may sometimes hear him groaning.'

Above: THE WREKIN, THE NEEDLE'S EYE C1960 W152057

Left: THE WREKIN, THE NEEDLE'S EYE 1895 35977

THE WREKIN *Telford, Shropshire*

137

WHITE HORSE HILL
Uffington, Oxfordshire

The most famous, and to many people the most beautiful of all white horses, the Uffington horse lies on the Berkshire Downs near Wantage. It is larger than all the other white horses that we know of, at 365ft in length. Its primitive and stylised design link it, through images on coins, with the ancient Iron Age tribe of the Atrebates, who ruled the area before the Roman invasion, and it may have been a tribal emblem or totem. It is possible, however, that it is not a horse at all – some schools of thought think that the thin, galloping figure with its almost bird-like head may be a dragon, or even a cat. The Uffington White Horse is close to several ancient earthworks and burial mounds, overlooking an area which has been known as the Vale of the White Horse for more than a thousand years. Close by is the flat-topped Dragon's Hill, where legend says that St George slew the dragon. 'Dragon' was a Celtic word used in ancient times to describe a leader; for instance, King Arthur's father – Uther 'Pendragon' was 'Head Dragon'. Therefore George the dragon slayer probably defeated a local warlord or warrior who may have been defending Dragon Hill, or abusing his power. It is said that the bare patches of ground on Dragon Hill are where the dragon's blood was spilled!

Above: UFFINGTON, DRAGON'S HILL C1960 U24004

Opposite above: UFFINGTON, WHITE HORSE HILL C1965 U24325

Opposite below: UFFINGTON, THE WHITE HORSE C1960 U24025R

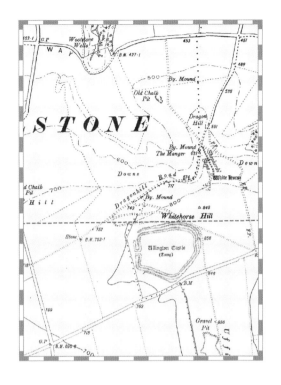

Scouring the white horse

The scouring of the horse, or in other words clearing away encroaching vegetation to keep its outlines clear, followed by a feast and celebrations, was first recorded in 1677, but it must have been a custom maintained long before that date. The scouring took place at regular intervals, probably at Midsummer or Michaelmas every seven years or so. Thomas Hughes, in his novel 'The Scouring of the White Horse' (1853), describes a sizeable country fair with many stalls and competitions, and the chasing of a wagon wheel rolled down the hill – this may be a folk memory of prehistoric rituals to do with the sun. He also describes the setting of the white horse in 'Tom Brown's Schooldays' (1857): 'Right up on the highest point, from which they say you can see eleven counties, they trenched round all the table-land, some twelve or fourteen acres, as was their custom, for they couldn't bear anybody to overlook them, and made their eyrie. The ground falls away rapidly on all sides. Was there ever such turf in the whole world? You sink up to your ankles at every step, and yet the spring of it is delicious. There is always a breeze in the 'camp' as it is called, and here it lies, just as the Romans left it … The pious King, that there might never be wanting a sign and a memorial to the country-side, carved out on the northern side of the chalk hill, under the camp, where it is most precipitous, the great Saxon white horse, which he who will may see from the railway, and which gives its name to the vale, over which it has looked these thousand years and more.'

THE BLOWING STONE
Kingston Lisle, Oxfordshire

KINGSTON LISLE, THE BLOWING STONE C1965 K86003

This 3ft-tall chunk of sarsen stone was brought into the village from its original site, which may have been on Kingstone Down, by the local blacksmith in the 18th century. The stone is pierced by a number of holes, one of which can be blown through to produce a loud bellow. Local legend says that the stone was used by King Alfred to summon the local militia to fight against the Danes at the Battle of Ashdown. By 1809 the smithy had become the Blowing Stone Inn, and for a small payment the landlord would perform upon the stone!

Three elements make up the Rollright Stones: the Whispering Knights, the King's Men, and the King Stone. These three elements are all of different dates, and this fact indicates that this was a sacred site over a very long period of time. Indeed, a rich body of folklore about the stones has endured until relatively recently; for instance, the Whispering Knights were said to tell the future, local people used to meet at the stones once a year for merrymaking, and in Tudor times there are reports of witches using the circle as a meeting place. As the great archaeologist Sir Arthur Evans (1851–1941) wrote: 'The folklore of which the Rollright Stones have become the centre is of the highest interest, and it would be difficult to find any English site in which it is more living at the present day. I have myself taken down from the lips of the country people in the immediate neighbourhood … a quantity of tales relating to the stones.' The Whispering Knights are in fact the remains of a Neolithic burial chamber of about 4,000BC. This photograph shows the King's Men, a large stone circle dating from around 2,000BC. Its integrity cannot be verified; there are today 73 stones that make up the circle, yet a drawing made in the 17th century by John Aubrey shows only 25 standing stones. Time and man have ravaged the limestone uprights, and in 1882 the circle was 'restored': the stones are not all original, some are the broken tops of stones, and others have been wrongly re-sited.

Above: CHIPPING NORTON, THE ROLLRIGHT STONES, THE KING'S MEN C1960 C288073

THE ROLLRIGHT STONES

Chipping Norton, Oxfordshire

Next to the circle is the railed King Stone, a large block of limestone about 2.5m high. It was erected to mark an early Bronze Age cemetery; excavations in 1979 found small mounds containing cremated remains around the stone. It is badly deformed by natural erosion over time and by people, who in times past used to chip pieces off as lucky talismans. This was considered to be a magical stone, and barren women would press their breasts against the stone in hope of a child.

Left:
CHIPPING NORTON,
THE ROLLRIGHT STONES,
THE KING STONE C1960 C288070

Jacquetta Hawkes, in her 'Guide to the Prehistoric and Roman Monuments in England and Wales' (1951), tells the legend of the origin of the stones:

'A king was setting out to conquer all England, but as he led his army up the hill at Rollright he met the witch to whom the land belonged. A few steps further and he would be on the crest with Long Compton visible in the valley on the other side; he was therefore delighted when the witch said:

> *Seven long strides shalt thou take.*
> *If Long Compton thou canst see*
> *King of England thou shalt be.*

And he himself cried out:

> *Stick, stock, stone,*
> *As King of England I shall be known.*

He took the seven strides, but he did not know of the existence of the long barrow,

and its extra height prevented him from seeing Long Compton. The witch, with the unfair triumph of supernatural powers, pronounced:

> *As Long Compton thou canst not see,*
> *King of England thou shalt not be,*
> *Rise up, stick, and stand still, stone,*
> *For King of England thou shalt be none;*
> *Thou and thy men hoar stones shall be*
> *And I myself an eldern tree.*

Immediately the king and his men were turned to stone, as so also were some treacherous followers who had been whispering plots together in the background; the witch obeyed her own prophecy and became an elder-tree.' Jacquetta Hawkes adds: 'Let the traveller, the seeker after antiquities, accept this lesson from Rollright: the past has left marks deep in the human mind as real as the tangible marks which we search out among our fields and hills.'

THE ROMAN ROAD

Sutton Coldfield, West Midlands

SUTTON COLDFIELD, THE ROMAN ROAD 2005 S339701K

The road running through Sutton Park is part of the route from the Roman fort at Metchley, Birmingham. The road surface (known as the 'agger'), the roadside ditches and even the pits where the stones were excavated to pave the road can still be seen, if you know where to look. Whilst turf protects much of the road, the gravel surface is still visible in short patches. The parallel ditch markers that guided the road builders and the quarries from which they were able to extract the stone are overgrown with heather and long grasses and it takes a sharp eye to realise that what you are looking at is evidence of Roman construction and not just uneven ground.

St Chad, the patron saint of Mercia, died of plague in AD672, and pilgrims soon began to visit his shrine. This famous illuminated book, written and decorated in the 8th century, is now kept in Lichfield Cathedral and was probably associated with St Chad's shrine. Judging by the style of the book, the artist who created the St Chad Gospels studied the Lindisfarne Gospels, which were produced on Holy Island in the early 8th century. However, he did not use the same text as the Lindisfarne Gospels, but a text preferred in monasteries founded by St Columba and his followers, which included Lichfield. The page we see here is the famous 'carpet page', a complex design incorporating a cross.

Above right: LICHFIELD, THE ST CHAD GOSPELS C1890 L45302

Below right: LICHFIELD CATHEDRAL, THE NAVE C1880 12830

ST CHAD   *Lichfield, Staffordshire*

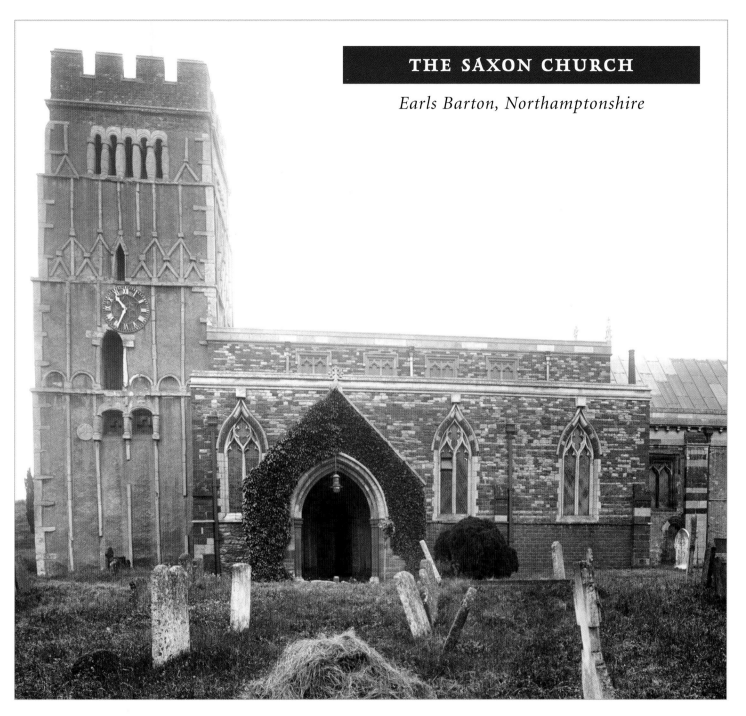

THE SAXON CHURCH

Earls Barton, Northamptonshire

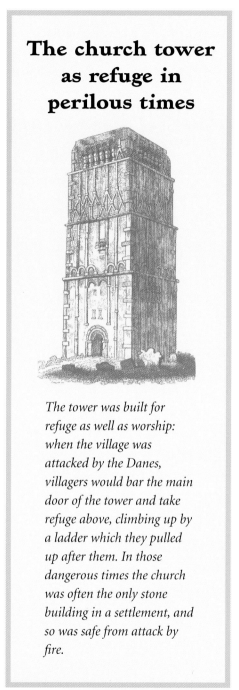

The church tower as refuge in perilous times

The tower was built for refuge as well as worship: when the village was attacked by the Danes, villagers would bar the main door of the tower and take refuge above, climbing up by a ladder which they pulled up after them. In those dangerous times the church was often the only stone building in a settlement, and so was safe from attack by fire.

Earls Barton is famous for its Church of All Saints, which has a Saxon tower of around AD970. The strip-like stonework on this church is an interesting feature, and was probably intended to resemble the timberwork of an earlier church. Notice too the typical Saxon long-and-short work (alternating perpendicular and horizontal stones) at the quoins of the tower, the small window openings (the ones at the top with baluster pillars are again typically Saxon), and the plaster rendering, an agreeable contrast to the exposed stone of the rest of the church. This is one of England's most important Anglo-Saxon monuments.

Above left:
EARLS BARTON, THE CHURCH 1922
72217

THE HORN DANCE — *Abbots Bromley, Staffordshire*

The Abbot's Bromley Horn Dance ritual dates back at least as far as 1226 – the first recorded performance was at the three-day Barthelmy Fair in that year. However, it is believed to be much older than that, and has survived down the centuries, continuing to flourish today in this Staffordshire village. The horns themselves have been carbon dated and are 1,000 years old. The dance is performed on Wakes Monday. The horns are collected from the church in the morning, and carried aloft, the dancers performing their ritual nowadays to music played on a melodeon.

Above: ABBOTS BROMLEY, THE HORN DANCE C1955 A165385P

A ten-mile dance round the village

The dancers – six Deer-men, a Fool, a Hobby Horse, a Bowman and Maid Marian – carry the horns around the village, stopping traffic and performing the dance many times. They trek up to ten miles, threading a path between the outlying farms and houses. Meanwhile, a jester strikes people in the crowd with a pig's bladder, which is said to encourage fertility.

The remains of Ratae Coritanorum, a regional capital in Roman Britain, and the major local centre for the Coritani tribe, lie adjacent to the superb Saxon church of St Nicholas in Leicester and are seen here in the centre of the photograph. Kathleen Kenyon performed the excavations here between 1936 and 1939; at first it was thought that these remains were part of the forum and basilica, but it is generally thought today that in fact what we see here was part of a large bath complex. The so-called Jewry Wall, 7.3m high, formed part of the exercise hall to the public bath. The remains are situated at the top of the High Street; today this is a park-like area surrounded by modern buildings.

Left: LEICESTER, THE ROMAN REMAINS C1955 L144053

Below: LEICESTER, THE ROMAN REMAINS AND JEWRY WALL C1955 L144069

THE HEMLOCK STONE

Stapleford, Nottinghamshire

This wind-eroded sandstone outcrop, about 30ft high, has attracted many legends. One story is that the Devil threw it at the now almost completely ruinous Lenton Priory.

Above left: STAPLEFORD, THE HEMLOCK STONE C1955   S718038

Above right: NOTTINGHAM, THE ROBIN HOOD CAVES 1893   33245

THE ROBIN HOOD CAVES

Nottingham

Beneath the city of Nottingham is a labyrinth of over 200 caves, which can now be explored by visitors on guided tours. Although the Robin Hood connection with Nottingham is more related to the fictional tales than a definite historical personage, the caves have been used for many purposes over Nottingham's long history. The first record of the caves appears in Asser's 'Life of King Alfred', written in AD900: Nottingham is called 'Tiggua Cobaucc', 'Place of Caves', and many of the caves date from Saxon times. The sandstone on which Nottingham stands is easy to excavate with basic tools and provided a dry environment with fresh water available from wells. The first cave houses were probably very simple, but later became much more elaborate, with two stories, carved stone staircases, and fireplaces.

The Nottingham caves were also used by craftsmen and traders for workshops and storage, including blacksmiths, fishgutters and butchers, and there was a medieval tannery here. The even temperature of the caves made them ideal for maltsters and brewers. The caves were still being used as dwellings in the 19th century, and they became air raid shelters during the Second World War.

ST ALBANS, THE ROMAN THEATRE AT VERULAMIUM C1959 S219

The Romans, when they established themselves in Britain after AD43, built the first Verulamium down the hillside from Prae Wood – Bluehouse Hill it is called today – towards the Ver, where it protected a ford; this first Verulamium was overrun during the insurrection of Boudicca in AD61 and many of the inhabitants were slaughtered. However, after the defeat of the British queen, the city quickly recovered and was rebuilt. A hundred years later, the city was destroyed by fire and again rebuilt, but this time in stone and to a very high standard. Many of the buildings had under-floor central heating systems (hypocausts), and one of these can still be seen today in a special display pavilion in Verulam Park. The city of over 200 acres, the third largest in Britain, was surrounded by a defensive wall over two miles long. It is thought there was a triumphal arch close to the south gate. There were numerous temples and civic buildings in the city, including a basilica.

In the centre of the city stood the theatre, built in the 2nd century, and one of only six theatres believed to have existed in Roman Britain. Excavated in the 1930s, this was found to have seated about 1,600 spectators and was used for plays, readings and, probably, civic meetings. The area around the theatre has also been thoroughly investigated and surveyed; many artefacts have been carefully conserved and are on display in the excellent Verulamium Museum opposite St Michael's Church.

Above: ST ALBANS, VERULAMIUM, THE ROMAN WALL C1955 S2043

ST ALBANS, THE ROMAN THEATRE AT VERULAMIUM C1955 S2045

Recycling and building a new town

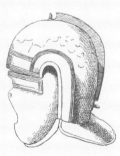

When the Romans left Britain in the early 5th century Verulamium fell into decay, and it became an enormous 'reclamation centre' where the materials were found to construct the abbey, churches and other buildings in the new town of St Albans (named after the 3rd-century British-born saint and martyr) which was starting to flourish nearby.

Roman Roads in Britain

During the period of Roman administration around 10,000 miles (16,000km) of roads were built in Britain, mainly to give easy access to the garrison towns placed strategically throughout the country. The Roman roads radiated out from Londinium, the area near present-day London Bridge. Certain sections of these roads appear to have been constructed on what were once prehistoric tracks, showing a continuity of use which in some cases continues to this day, since many modern roads were built over the Roman routes. The imperial roads were so well made that many of them were still in use during the medieval period; King Edward the Confessor passed laws to ensure that the principal Roman routes of Watling Street, the Fosse Way, Hikenith (the Icknield Way) and Ermine Street were kept clear from sea to sea.

Colchester's High Street lies along the central axis of the Roman legionary fortress that was built here in AD43, the year of the Roman invasion of Britain. In the early stages of the Roman conquest, Emperor Claudius himself came to Colchester (Camulodunum), where he personally received the surrender of the native tribes. His triumphal procession into the town included war elephants. According to Tacitus, the Roman historian, the first Roman settlement at Colchester was built as a colony for retired soldiers, along with a temple dedicated to the Emperor Claudius. The town was attacked and burned by the forces of Boudicca, who led the last British revolt against Roman rule in around AD61. The inhabitants took refuge in the temple of Claudius, but were burnt to death or massacred. The later Norman castle keep was built around the podium of the ruined temple in the 11th century.

The Castle Museum in Colchester contains a fascinating collection of items from everyday life in Roman times, including a terracotta baby's feeding bottle dating from about AD180. There are also some touching terracotta toys, a boar, a bull and other animals, which were found buried in a baby's grave. In December 2004 archaeologists working on a housing development at Colchester unearthed what they believe is almost certainly the only known Roman circus – or chariot-racing circuit – in Britain. The site was the subject of a special 'Time Team' TV programme in May 2005. A circus was the largest entertainment building in the Roman world, and Colchester's was about 70m wide and 350m long.

After Boudicca's revolt, the Romans rebuilt Colchester within a hundred years. Consequently it was one of the first Romano-British towns to have complete city walls. There are still many visible remains of the Roman walls in present-day Colchester; one of these is Balkerne Gate. This was the great west gate, the entry into the town from the London road, and the grandest of all the town's entrances. The importance of this west gate was emphasised by a stone-faced triumphal arch with vehicle carriageways, each 17ft wide. The rest of the gate had a pedestrian way each side and a quadrant bastion, which contained a north and south guardroom. The whole gate, 117ft across, was set forward from the line of the wall. Much of it still survives today, including the south pedestrian way (still in use), and its guardroom bastion. The north bastion, pedestrian way and parts of the triumphal arch foundations remain under (and supporting) the Hole in the Wall pub.

Opposite: COLCHESTER, THE CASTLE 1891 28215

Above: COLCHESTER, THE CASTLE INTERIOR 1895 35504

Shakespeare's 'Cymbeline' tells the story of the British king Cunobelinus, whose chief settlement was Colchester – he ruled from approximately AD7 to AD40. Under his leadership the Catuvellauni tribe overran the territory of the neighbouring Trinovantes and conquered the area now known as Kent. By the end of his life, Cunobelinus controlled most of south-east Britain, and the Roman historian Suetonius called him 'the King of the Britons'. After the death of King Cunobelinus in about AD40, the territory around Colchester was ruled jointly by his sons Caractacus and Togodumnus. These two powerful kings led the British opposition to the Roman invasion of Britain in AD43. They were unable to organise a coherent opposition to the imperial might, and Caratacus retreated, going first to Wales and then to the north of England, where he was betrayed to the Romans by Cartimandua, Queen of the Brigantes.

Above: COLCHESTER, THE ROMAN WALL 1892   31531

The famous Sutton Hoo ship burial was excavated in 1939, in an area of 18 Saxon burial mounds. Beneath the largest mound were the remains of a 30ft oak ship. No body was found at the time of the excavation, but recent research shows that there

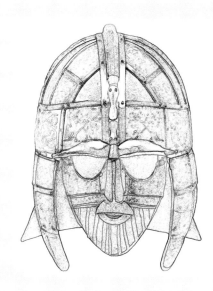

may well have been a body buried with the ship, which was completely destroyed by the acid soil. The ship was full of grave goods, many of gold and silver, and included this famous helmet, made of gilded bronze, which can now be seen in the British Museum. The finds included weapons, coins, armour, and cups, as well as garments and textiles, all of the finest craftsmanship. The opulence of these objects signifies a grave of someone of the greatest importance, certainly someone from the Wuffingas royal family, which settled in East Anglia from Sweden in the late 5th century. Who was buried here? The dates of the coins found in the grave range between AD575 and AD620. There are four major East Anglian kings known to have ruled around this time – Raedwald, Eorpwald, Sigebert and Ecric – and Raedwald is probably the most likely candidate. There is an evocative desciption of the raising of a burial mound in the epic Anglo-Saxon poem 'Beowulf', probably written down around AD750 from an earlier oral tradition:

'Upon the headland the Geats erected a broad high tumulus plainly visible to distant seamen ... within the barrow they placed collars, brooches and all the trappings which they had plundered from the treasure hoard. They buried the gold and left that princely treasure to the earth where it remains'.

Above: AN ARTIST'S IMPRESSION OF THE SUTTON HOO HELMET   F6024

BURGH CASTLE

Great Yarmouth, Norfolk

Great Yarmouth is intimately connected with the North Sea. In Roman times the very ground on which the town now stands was under water. Burgh Castle, just west of Great Yarmouth, was a Saxon Shore fort (see Portchester Castle, page 92, for an explanation of what these were) built by the Romans on what was then a peninsula looking out on the estuary of the River Waveney. Three sides of the fort remain; the massive walls were over 3m thick and 4.6m high with projecting bastions, clearly visible in this photograph. The flint rubble in the walls has eroded more than the better-bonded courses of red tiles, leaving the curious wavy layered effect. As at Portchester, the enclosure was later used by the Normans as the bailey of a castle.

Opposite: BURGH CASTLE, THE WATCH TOWER AND THE CASTLE WALLS C1955 B498020

Above right: SHERINGHAM, THE VIEW FROM THE ROMAN ENCAMPMENT 1894 33320

Below right: SHERINGHAM, THE ROMAN ENCAMPMENT 1922 72654

THE ROMAN ENCAMPMENT — *Sheringham, Norfolk*

Legend has it that the Romans billeted here so that their enemies could easily be seen; they lit signal fires to alert troops in the area. A Roman kiln has been excavated here.

ST WITHBURGA'S WELL

East Dereham, Norfolk

Withburga was a Saxon princess, one of the four daughters of Anna, King of the Angles, and sister of Etheldreda, founder of the monastery at Ely. Tradition says that St Withburga died in AD743, which would have made her very old, and she was buried in St Nicholas's churchyard until a shrine could be built. When her body was moved to the shrine, her coffin was opened, and her body still looked as it had on the day she died. Indeed, legend says that when one man touched her cheek, the maiden saint blushed. Two hundred years later, King Edgar and the monks of Ely decided that Withburga should lie with her sisters at Ely. The villagers were reluctant to let her go; but when in AD974 her remains were taken to Ely Cathedral, the spring that feeds St Withburga's Well gushed forth from her previous burial place in Dereham, a recompense to the villagers for the loss of their saint. Pilgrims continued to visit Dereham, and St Withburga's holy water was said to have healing properties. In the 18th century a bath-house was built over the spring in the hope that Dereham would become a spa town. It was never successful, however, and was pulled down in about 1880, when the railing we see in the photographs was put up. Over the years the ivy and ferns have been replaced by shrubs and garden plants.

Left: EAST DEREHAM, ST WITHBURGA'S WELL
1922   72561A

Below: EAST DEREHAM, THE CHURCH, ST WITHBURGA'S
WELL 1893   33307

East Dereham's town sign that tells Withburga's story

EAST DEREHAM, THE TOWN SIGN C1954 D25100

This town sign tells Withburga's story: Withburga established a nunnery at Dereham in AD654, the first Christian settlement in the area. The nuns and the villagers were very poor, but one night the Virgin Mary appeared to Withburga, and told her that two deer would come to be milked so that all could have drink, butter and cheese. However, the reeve of the village was jealous of Withburga; he came after the deer with his dogs, but he fell from his horse and died instantly.

THE UNICURSAL MAZE

Hilton, Cambridgeshire

Children have played on this maze on the village green for centuries. It is thought that it was re-cut from an older maze by William Sparrow in 1660 to commemorate the restoration to the throne of Charles II, and it is still beautifully maintained. One of only eight mazes surviving in Britain, it is of the unicursal type – there are no dead ends, and the narrow grass track leads circuitously to the centre without any deviation. Mazes, or labyrinths, are very ancient devices, and were often used on early Christian sites, either as aids to contemplation or during acts of penance, when monks would follow the course of the maze on their hands and knees.

Left: HILTON, THE UNICURSAL MAZE C1955 H440029

157

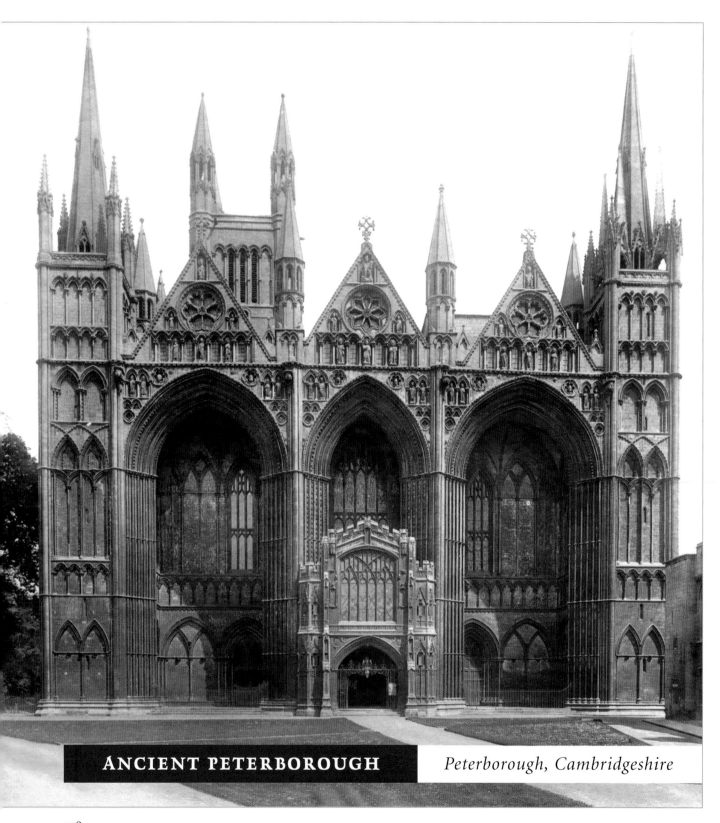

Peterborough stands on ancient foundations; excavations have revealed a thatched hut dating from about 3,500BC. There was a Roman town and fortress here, and later the Saxons established both a town and an abbey. The abbey church was destroyed and rebuilt several times, and only a small section of the foundations of the Saxon church remains, under the south transept of the present building, although some fragments of Saxon carving can still be seen. The abbey church, much as we see it today, was consecrated in 1238 and became a cathedral in the 16th century; it remains Peterborough's chief glory.

Above: PETERBOROUGH, THE ENTRANCE TO THE FOUNDATIONS OF THE SAXON CHURCH C1955 P47062

Left: PETERBOROUGH CATHEDRAL, THE WEST FRONT 1904 51551

ANCIENT PETERBOROUGH *Peterborough, Cambridgeshire*

When the Roman soldiers of the Ninth Legion marched toward the River Witham as it flowed slowly through the gap in the limestone ridge escarpment now known as the Lincoln Edge, they saw little apart from trees and a few wreaths of wispy smoke rising above a collection of Iron Age huts grouped by the side of a shallow lake. Crossing the river and making the steep climb out of the valley, they were clearly struck by the defensive possibilities of the hilltop location. This would be the place where the Romans built a great legionary fortress protecting the meeting point of the Roman roads of what is now referred to as Ermine Street and the earlier Fosse Way. The fortress, capable of housing some 5,000 men, was certainly complete by AD68. However, the formal military presence was short-lived. Soon after AD86 the Romans designated the settlement as a colonia, an important town for retired soldiers. The new settlement came to be known as Lindum Colonia (the Celtic word for a pool or lake is 'lind'). But it is from this Roman renaming that we arrive at today's name for the city, Lincoln.

The upper part of Steep Hill exactly overlies the line of the Roman road known as Ermine Street. One of the first phases of activity in building the new colonia was the creation of the streets. Several of the surviving fort streets, in what was to become known as the upper city, were provided with drains or sewers and then resurfaced. These streets followed a grid pattern, which then extended outside the fort walls to the south on either side of Ermine Street (now the High Street) as far as the river.

A ROMAN FORTRESS | *Lincoln, Lincolnshire*

Left: LINCOLN, STEEP HILL 1923 74640P

159

At the beginning of the second century AD work started on rebuilding the walls of the upper city. The line of the new walls, built of local limestone, followed that of the earlier fort. The gates were also rebuilt in stone. One such gate still stands as a unique survival from this period, the Newport Arch, which is located at the northern end of Bailgate (25660, above). What makes it unique, at least in Britain, is its continued use for road traffic, though this was nearly its undoing in 1964 when an over-height lorry attempted to pass beneath it, causing considerable damage. The building on the left has been demolished since this photograph was taken in 1890, allowing the pavement to be moved outside of the archway.

Top: LINCOLN, THE NEWPORT ARCH 1890 25660

The baths complex of Roman Lincoln was located in the north-east corner of the upper city and consisted of a series of heated and unheated rooms, plunge-baths and a gymnasium area. Bathhouses required a substantial supply of water if they were to function properly; consequently extra water was brought to Lincoln from outside the city. Lincoln's aqueduct was little more than a ceramic pipe 15cm in diameter encased in hydraulic concrete, but it served its purpose. Possibly drawing water from the Roaring Meg spring-head to the north-east of the city, or more likely from the distant Wolds, the aqueduct was carried over a small valley on a series of regular stone-built piers before being buried underground on its approach to the city. At least one branch of the aqueduct arrived at the north wall just to the east of the Newport Arch and fed a large masonry tank capable of holding around 12,000 litres of water. The position and partial remains of this water tank can still be seen in a garden to the north of East Bight.

Initially the buildings of the lower city spread across the hillside and waterside to both the east and west, but all broadly respected a street grid that drew its orientation from that of the upper city. In the late 2nd or early 3rd century a decision was taken, probably in response to some imminent danger, to enclose the lower city behind substantial defensive walls. The walls of the lower city were clearly pierced in several places by gates, including the points where the wall crosses the line of modern day West Parade and Monks Road. The most important gate must have been that across Ermine Street to the south. This may in fact represent the site of an earlier triumphal arch that greeted visitors to the city even before the walls were built. In the southern length of the western wall a new gateway was inserted some time in the later 4th century. This reused monumental stonework possibly taken from the adjacent cemetery.

While the core of the early civilian settlement was located within the boundary of the earlier fortress, further areas of occupation spilled down the hillside and extended south along either side of Ermine Street, now the High Street. Dividing the two 'cities' was the upper city's south wall, pierced in its centre by the upper south gate, the remains of which can be seen in L49702k, above. From this point the street drops sharply down the hillside. The Romans overcame the severe incline by paving the street with large stone steps. On either side of these, great retaining walls supported terraces, on which were constructed further public buildings, including perhaps a theatre. The steps would have hindered the passage of wheeled vehicles, so a zigzag diversion was constructed to the east. This diversion still exists in part in the form of Well Lane and Danesgate, and continues to provide a marginally less strenuous ascent for those who want to bypass the steepest part of Steep Hill.

Ermine Street

If you had asked a Roman inhabitant of Lincoln the way to Ermine Street they would not have known what you were talking about! The name 'Ermine' actually dates from the Saxon period, and is thought to have been associated with a group of people known as the Earningas who lived in a part of Cambridgeshire through which the road passed.

Left: LINCOLN, REMAINS OF THE WESTERN SIDE OF THE ROMAN UPPER SOUTH GATE ON STEEP HILL 2004 L49702K

Above: LINCOLN, REMAINS OF THE ROMAN LOWER CITY WEST GATE 2004 L49703K

The history of Grimsby begins with 'The Lay of Havelok the Dane'. This poem, the earliest known version of which dates back to 1170, tells the tale of a Danish fisherman named Grim, who, legend says, was responsible for the founding of the settlement of Grimsby by his kindness to Havelok.

Havelok, a hero of medieval romance, was the orphan son of Birkabein, the King of Denmark. As a young boy Havelok was cast adrift on the sea by his evil and treacherous guardian Godard, and doomed to a watery grave. His raft bore Havelok to the coast of Lincolnshire, where the fisherman Grim found and adopted him, raising him as his own son. Havelok is reputed to have helped Grim distribute and sell fish; by virtue of his phenomenal strength, he could manhandle enormous fish baskets that were beyond the strength of ordinary men. When a period of drought and famine forced Havelok to seek work further afield, he joined the court of Alsi, the King of Lindsey, at Lincoln as a porter and scullion in the royal kitchens, where he soon became renowned for his feats of strength.

HAVELOK THE DANE

Grimsby, Lincolnshire

Above left: GRIMSBY, THE HAVELOCK STONE 2004 G60702K

Above right: GRIMSBY, THE STATUE OF GRIM 2004 G60703K

Goldburga, the princess daughter of King Athelwold of England, lived in nearby Lincoln as the ward of King Alsi, who had promised to marry Goldburga to the strongest and fairest man in the land. At a stone-throwing contest, Havelok managed to lift a great stone higher and hurl it further than anyone else, and thus he won the hand of his wife. Havelok eventually returned to his homeland, where he became king of both Denmark and of the part of England held in trust by King Alsi for Goldburga. In the fullness of time, King Havelok is said to have financially rewarded the ageing Grim for his kindness, and with this money the fisherman built Grim's town or Grimsby.

A statue of Grim the fisherman (G60703k, left) stands today in the grounds of the Grimsby College of Technology. The Havelock Stone (G60702k) sits outside the Welholme Gallery in Grimsby, though whether this is the very stone reputedly thrown by Havelok to win the hand of Goldburga is for romantics to believe.

The strategic importance of the site now occupied by Chester was realised by the Romans during their campaigns against the Brigantes and the Welsh. The site was on the north bank of the Dee at the lowest bridging point before the estuary. The fortress covered 56 acres, surrounded by an outer ditch and a turfed rampart topped by a wooden palisade, together with wooden gatehouses and towers. Capable of holding a legion (initially the Second Legion, then the Twentieth Legion), the huge fortress was completed in AD79–80, but at some time around AD100 reconstruction work began to make Deva, as it was called, a more permanent establishment. Rome was here to stay, and occupied the site for over 300 years. The medieval town walls (among the most complete in Britain) largely follow the line of the Roman ones. This photograph (20616) shows the remains of a Roman hypocaust, the heating system for a Roman bath, discovered in Bridge Street in 1863 and subsequently relocated to the gardens by the Water Tower, part of the medieval defences.

THE WATER TOWER AND THE ROMAN HYPOCAUST

Chester, Cheshire

REMAINS OF A ROMAN BATH DISCOVERED IN BRIDGE ST 1863

CHESTER, THE WATER TOWER AND THE ROMAN HYPOCAUST 1888 20616

Chester's ancient walls

'But in spite of this sturdy origin, much of which is buried in the well-trodden soil of the ages, it is the gentlest and least offensive of ramparts; it completes its long irregular curve without a frown or menace in all its disembattled stretch. The earthy deposit of time has, indeed, in some places climbed so high about its base that it amounts to no more than a causeway of modest dimensions. It has everywhere, however, a rugged outer parapet and a broad hollow flagging, wide enough for two strollers abreast. Thus equipped, it wanders through its adventurous circuit; now sloping, now bending, now broadening into a terrace, now narrowing into an alley, now swelling into an arch, now dipping into steps, now passing some thorn-screened garden, and now reminding you that it was once a more serious matter than all this by the extrusion of a rugged, ivy-smothered tower. Its final hoary humility is enhanced, to your mind, by the freedom with which you may approach it from any point in the town. Every few steps, as you go, you see some little court or alley boring toward it through the close-pressed houses.'

HENRY JAMES 1872

THE HYPOCAUST AT CHESTER

THE BRIDESTONES   *Timbersbrook, Cheshire*

The Bridestones are the remains of a Neolithic chambered tomb, believed to date back to around 3,000BC, and are often described as Cheshire's only megalithic monument. The tomb was aligned east to west, and originally had a covering mound and two other chambers. All that is left today is the main chamber, but the tomb is believed to have had a horned cairn and crescent-shaped forecourt. It was excavated in the 18th century.

There are several theories as to how the tomb acquired its name, one being that it relates to the ancient fertility goddess Bride. Another old legend says that the stones are the petrified members of a wedding party, whilst Jacqueline Simpson's 'Folklore of the Welsh Border' (1976) notes a story from Ingram's 'Companion into Cheshire' (1947) that a Viking was buried here with his bride, a local Saxon girl. Yet another explanation is that the name is the result of a wedding that was held here in the 1930s!

Above: TIMBERSBROOK, THE BRIDESTONES C1955   T219010

THE SAXON CROSSES

Sandbach, Cheshire

THE OLD CROSS

Gawsworth, Cheshire

Above: GAWSWORTH, THE OLD CROSS 1897   40466

This photograph shows all that is left of an early medieval preaching cross. The remains comprise two steps, with a stepped socket stone and a fragment of the shaft. Preaching crosses were erected from Saxon times onwards, usually at a cross-roads, and here monks or travelling friars would preach, and perhaps baptise the people of village or town. Ancient preaching crosses like this, usually set high on steps, can be seen in villages, towns and cities all over Britain, often now known as market crosses.

Despite the fact that so many towns and villages in Britain were founded in Saxon times, few have any tangible reminders of their Saxon history left other than perhaps their names. In Sandbach, however, it is possible to see the shafts of two stunningly beautiful Saxon crosses. The taller one is covered with scenes from the life of Christ, whilst the smaller one is thought to depict scenes from the life of King Penda of Mercia (whose territory this once was). He was converted to Christianity some time around AD653.

Left: SANDBACH, ANCIENT SAXON CROSSES C1955   S489016

THE DOVE HOLES — *Dovedale, Derbyshire*

Dovedale's name is derived from the Celtic word 'dubh', meaning 'black, dark'. Millions of years ago this area was a coral reef, which formed the limestone of the dale. The two great gaping maws of the Dove Holes are thought to have been carved out of the limestone of the Nab, at the northern end of Dovedale, by the action of Ice Age meltwater. Looking like archetypal cavemen's dwellings, the Dove Holes have indeed revealed traces of prehistoric use: they were probably used about 14,000 years ago, during the Ice Age, and again much later during the Neolithic era. In Roman times, shepherds may have sheltered here. The larger of these big, shallow caves is 60ft wide and 30ft high.

Tall lime-stone cliffs, splintered into countless fantastic forms

'The river is a shallow, sparkling stream, with many a pool dear to the angler, and hurrying down, babbling over pebbles, and broken in its course by many a tiny waterfall. On both sides rise tall lime-stone cliffs, splintered into countless fantastic forms – rocky walls, towers, and pinnacles, and in one place a natural archway near the summit, leading to the uplands beyond. And all up the sloping sides, and wherever root-hold could be obtained on pinnacle and crag, were clustered shrubs and trees of every shade of foliage, with the first touch of autumn to heighten the exquisite variety by tints which as yet suggested only afar off the thought of decay. The solitude of the scene served but to enhance its loveliness.' THE REV SAMUEL MANNING 1885

Left: DOVEDALE, THE DOVE HOLES AND CAPTAIN'S ROCK 1894   34258   *Above:* DOVEDALE, THE DOVE HOLES C1864   2084

SAXON CROSSES

Derbyshire and Lancashire

Above: EYAM, THE SAXON CROSS 1896 37815

Right: HOPE, THE SAXON CROSS AND THE
SUNDIAL 1932 85264

The vigorously carved Saxon cross which stands in Eyam's churchyard is thought to date from around the 7th century (37815, opposite far left); the carvings depict a mixture of pagan and Christian symbols. Similar in style to the crosses at Bakewell, it was originally a preaching cross set out in the countryside. At some point it was damaged at the top of its shaft, and today it presents a somewhat truncated appearance. Eyam's church is thought to stand on Saxon foundations, but what we can see today dates from the 13th and 14th centuries. On Eyam Moor above the village are many ancient remains from the Bronze Age. Eyam is famous today as the village which went into voluntary quarantine when the plague was imported from London in 1665.

The old market cross, or preaching cross (right of photograph 85264, opposite page), now used as a sundial, stands in the churchyard opposite the headless Saxon cross (left of photograph), which is thought to date from the 9th century; it is covered with fine interlacing knotwork.

There are two fine Anglian crosses in Whalley's churchyard (42932 and 42934, left), and a third Anglian shaft with a head that is a later addition. The carved pattern on the cross shown in 42932 may possibly represent a Tree of Life.

Far left: WHALLEY, AN ANCIENT CROSS IN THE CHURCHYARD 1899 42934

Left: WHALLEY, AN ANCIENT CROSS IN THE CHURCHYARD 1899 42932

THE ROMAN BATH-HOUSE

Lancaster, Lancashire

LANCASTER, THE ROMAN BATH-HOUSE 2004 L10701K

I t was about AD70 when the first Roman commander would have looked out from the earliest of a succession of forts sited on the top of the hill where Lancaster's castle and St Mary's Priory Church now stand. The Roman fort at what is now Lancaster was not a major fort, but an auxiliary one; it was built on a drumlin, or ridge, left by a retreating glacier at the end of the last Ice Age, and stood above the lowest crossing point of the River Lune. Beside the fort a civilian settlement grew up; excavations here in 1973–74 found a building, probably an inn, with a bath-house - this had been demolished in about AD330 to make room for a new fort. The remains of the Roman bath-house are still to be seen in the field to the right when walking from the castle past the church and down to the river.

The Roman name of the fort is not known, but the name Lancaster itself is derived from the river name, 'Lune' or 'Loyne', and 'castra', the Roman for 'camp'.

St Patrick himself is said to have been shipwrecked on Heysham Head; years later, monks came from his monastic foundation in Ireland and built this chapel in his memory. It dates from Saxon times, from the 8th century, and one of the reasons it survived so long in such an exposed spot is the mortar, which was made from ground-up sea shells, heated and mixed with boiling water to give a cement-like substance. It is the only example left in England of a single-cell Saxon chapel. Originally it measured 24ft by 8ft, with walls nearly 3ft thick.

Left: HEYSHAM HEAD, ST PATRICK'S CHAPEL RUINS 1888 21071P

Above: HEYSHAM, STONE COFFINS 1912 64229

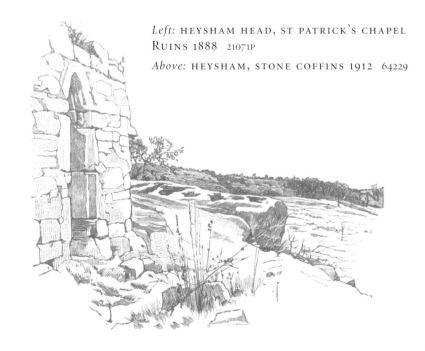

ST PATRICK'S CHAPEL
Heysham, Lancashire

These unique and mysterious stone coffins are near St Patrick's Chapel. Any explanations about these resting places cut into the rock can only be pure speculation. There are six here, and two more by the chapel door. They were cut during the Dark Ages with primitive tools, and may possibly have been used for burial more than once – the Vikings may have plundered the graves and thrown out the original corpses, and then perhaps the graves were used again when Christianity was restored. Carbon tests of the bones found in the coffins date from the 900s, yet the coffins are very much earlier.

Above: HEYSHAM, STONE COFFINS 1891   28595   *Below:* HEYSHAM, THE PARISH CHURCHYARD, THE HOGBACK STONE 1912   64232

This stone marked the grave of a Viking warrior for over 1,000 years; it is from the 10th century. He had converted to Christianity, but although one side of the stone is carved with Christian symbols, the other side represent the pagan Viking heaven, Valhalla. In 1961 the hogback stone was taken inside the church for protection against the weather, and against too many visitors running their hands over the stone. Though there are other hogback stones in Britain, this is the finest and best preserved.

THE MEAYLL CIRCLE

Cregneish, Isle of Man

CREGNEISH, THE MEAYLL CIRCLE 1897 39904

At the south end of the Isle of Man are a group of low hills, the Mull or Meayll (the name possibly derives from the Celtic 'meall', 'round hill'). In their fascinating account of their 1893 excavations here (to be found in 'Manks Antiquities', 2nd ed 1914), Professor W A Herdman and P M K Kermode speculate that this area was 'the last refuge in the south part of the Isle of Man of the pre-Celtic race'. Here they found at least three settlements, each containing up to 16 dwellings, in which they found charcoal, pottery fragments, and flint tools; the remarkable stone circle (built, like the settlements, in the local slate) was the ritual burial place common to all the settlements. The stone circle itself is a highly unusual design, 'formed', say Herdman and Kermode, 'of six symmetrically arranged sets of cists or stone chambers, each set – for which we propose the term 'tritaph' – being composed of one radial cist and two tangentially placed'; the diameter of the circle is about 55ft, and outside the circle is a circular bank. Within the cists were found fragments of over 20 pottery vessels, which contained cremated remains, flint tools and arrowheads. Judging by the pottery, which was Bronze Age in style, and the flint tools, it seemed probable to the excavators that the people who lived in the settlements and built the stone circle lived at a time of transition between the Neolithic era and the Bronze Age; also, 'the size and nature of the cists, the presence of the numerous quartz pebbles, the buried weapons and implements deposited with the ashes, all would seem to indicate the funeral rites of a people imbued with some religious ideas, however primitive.'

In the cist the excavators found some round white quartz pebbles from the beach; Herdman and Kermode wonder whether this is 'the origin of the superstitious dislike the natives still have to the use of the 'clagh-bane' or 'white stone'. Fishermen, for instance, will refuse to go to sea in a boat which has a white stone in the ballast.'

173

PEEL CASTLE

Isle of Man

The castle on St Patrick's Isle at Peel dates from between c1098-1103, when Magnus Barefoot built a timber fort there. The bulk of the surviving fortifications date from the time of Thomas, 1st Earl of Derby, and were constructed between 1460–1504 as a defence against Scottish raiders. A few years ago a 9th-century woman's grave was excavated on St Patrick's Isle. Although in a Christian cemetery, she had been buried with grave goods: comb, knife, chatelaine, spit (for roasting) and a goose wing (used for brushing out an oven). The most spectacular item, however, was a necklace with a wide variety of beads representing all areas of the known Viking world: a chain of memories rather like a souvenir charm bracelet.

Built in the Irish style, the round tower at Peel Castle (8597, above left) dates from the 10th or 11th century, and would have been used as a place of refuge during raids by pirates or Vikings. It is built from local red sandstone and stands 50ft high. Originally it would have had a conical stone roof, but this was replaced by the crenellated top many centuries ago.

Above left: PEEL CASTLE C1876 8597

Below left: PEEL CASTLE 1893 33047

TYNWALD HILL
St John's, Isle of Man

In around AD870, Tynwald Hill was selected by the Isle of Man Vikings as a suitable location, or 'vollr', to hold their open-air assembly, the 'Thing', held annually on Old Midsummer's Day (the name Tynwald derives from Thingvollr). Here freemen settled disputes, and laws for the forthcoming year were announced. Ever since then, Tynwald, the Manx parliament, has met here every year on 5 July. The ceremony has hardly changed at all in 1,000 years. Tynwald is unique – no other parliament in the world has met continuously for so long.

Above: ST JOHN'S, TYNWALD HILL 1903 50668

RUNIC CROSSES

Kirk Braddan, Isle of Man

The Isle of Man was settled by the Vikings in the 9th century. As the Vikings became Christian they adopted and adapted the Celtic crosses, and often added pagan images to them with inscriptions in runes. On a cross the runes are normally inscribed on a flat edge and read from the bottom to the top. Runes are generally thought of as Scandinavian, but some of the letters bear more than a little resemblance to our alphabet. The tall slender Kirk Braddan Cross is a beautiful example of Viking art in the Mammen style (named from a place in Denmark). It has interlaced dragons on its faces and a runic inscription on the edge.

Crosses and pagan legends

Many Viking age crosses in the Isle of Man have scenes of animals and people. Others show the Scandinavian pagan gods, such as Odin or Thor, or scenes from the Sigurd legend which was used by Wagner as the basis for his Ring cycle of operas. All the crosses in this photograph (right) and a very large Celtic interlace cross are now housed inside the church.

Above: KIRK BRADDAN, RUNIC CROSSES 1893 33020

The village of Maughold is one of a number of places on the Isle of Man named after Celtic saints. The legend of Maughold is that he was a pirate or brigand, who, seeing the error of his ways, allowed himself to be cast adrift in a leather boat, his arms and legs shackled. The boat drifted ashore on the Isle of Man, and Maughold told his story to the local bishop. He became a hermit and the fame of his piety spread. It was Maughold who gave the veil of virginity to St Bridget when she visited him here in AD498.

On the 14th-century pillared cross in Maughold (36736, right) is one of the two earliest surviving representations of the three legs which appear on the coat of arms of the Isle of Man. (The other is on the Manx Sword of State, which Olaf Godreson is said to have owned c1230). The device was used as early as 1310 by Henry de Bello Morte, Lord of Man. It may possibly derive from a triple knot design used by the Norse-Irish kings of Dublin.

Maughold's single-chambered keeills

As well as the cross there are also three examples of keeills at Maughold, one of which can be seen in the background of photograph 36736. Keeills are early Christian single-chambered chapels, nearly 200 of which are known to have existed. They were constructed with wattle and daub or stone walls with thatched roofs. Some had a window and/or an altar at the eastern end; the door was at the western end.

Above: MAUGHOLD, THE VILLAGE 1895 36733

Right: MAUGHOLD, THE CROSS 1895 36736

THE CROSS *Maughold, Isle of Man*

177

SÁXON CROSSES, THE SWÁSTIKÁ STONE

Ilkley, Yorkshire

The three fine and justly celebrated Celtic-style crosses in 7290 (left) – now kept inside All Saints' Church – are marked with pre-Christian symbols and some later carvings. It is believed that they were originally used as grave markers, or as markers for the spot where the Gospel would be preached before the church was built. The central pillar dates from AD850, and its carvings depict the four evangelists, Matthew, Mark, Luke and John.

Rombalds Moor near Ilkley (67342, above) is rich in prehistoric remains, including stone circles, cairns, and many carved rocks. Overlooking Ilkley is the Swastika Stone, so called because of its engraved design, the outline of a swastika with indentations inside the outline; it is similar to other Celtic designs, and it is thought that this dates the carving to the Iron Age, later than the numerous other carvings in the area. The swastika, infamous now thanks to its 20th-century associations, is in fact an ancient design which appears all over the world. It is said that its name derives from the Sanskrit word for well-being, and that the symbol means good fortune, or perhaps even fertility.

Left: ILKLEY, THE SAXON CROSSES IN THE CHURCHYARD C1874 7290
Above: ILKLEY, THE SWASTIKA STONE 1916 67342

THE DRUID'S ALTAR   *Bingley, Yorkshire*

The Druid's Altar is a natural large millstone grit formation on the edge of, and overlooking, the Aire valley conurbation, with Bradford to the east and to the west the eastern end of the Yorkshire Dales. The top of the rock bears cup and ring marks; these prehistoric carvings of concentric rings and channels are found mainly in the north of England, Scotland and Ireland, and there has been much speculation over their meaning. Are they mazes, or maps of the stars, or representations of burial mounds? Or are they sundials, or simply part of a game? Local antiquarians have theorised that the cobbled way running from the Brown Cow Inn towards the site is an old processional route walked as part of ancient ceremonies.

Above: BINGLEY, THE DRUID'S ALTAR 1894 34759

179

THE WELL — *Settle, Yorkshire*

Like many villages founded on limestone, Settle has its ebbing and flowing well. This is a spring which issues from the limestone as it hits impervious rocks beneath the limestone, ebbing and flowing thanks to a natural siphon in the rock. Michael Drayton, in his great topographical poem 'Polyolbion' (1622), recounts the legend of a nymph chased by a satyr. Exhausted and out of breath, she prayed to the gods for rescue, and they turned her into this well – its ebb and flow are due to her panting. More recently, there was a tradition of mixing the well water with liquorice and drinking it on Easter Day.

Above: SETTLE, THE EBBING AND FLOWING WELL 1921 71326

180

The satyr and the nymph

'At Gigglewick, where I a fountain can you show
That eight times a day is said to ebb and flow
Who sometime was a nymph, and in the mountains high
Of Craven, whose blue heads for caps put on the sky,
Amongst the Oreads there, and Sylvans made abode
(It was ere human foot upon these hills had trod)
Of all the mountain kind, and, since she was most fair
It was a Satyr's chance to see her silver hair
Flow loosely at her back, as up a cliffe she clame,
Her beauties noting well, her features, and her frame.
And after her he goes; which when she did espy
Before him like the wind the nimble nymph doth fly;
They hurry down the rocks, o'er hill and dale they drive;
To take her he doth strain, t'outstrip him she doth strive,
As one his kind that knew, and greatly feared his rape,
And to the topick gods by praying to escape,
They turned her to a spring, which as she then did pant,
When wearied with her cause her breath grew wonderous
    scant
Even as the fearful nymph, then thick and short did blow,
Now made by them a spring, so doth she ebb and flow.'

MICHAEL DRAYTON, 'POLYOLBION' (1622)

COVERDALE, DROVERS' CRAG 1926 79050

The Yorkshire Dales are criss-crossed by a network of ancient drovers' roads, like this one in Coverdale, a quiet dale which runs into the lower reaches of Wensleydale. Drovers' roads are usually characterised by their width. Large herds of cattle, sometimes from as far away as Scotland, were driven down them by generations of drovers to markets in the lowlands.

Photograph 65471 (left) shows the ancient hanging woodland clinging to limestone rock on the south bank of the River Swale just west of Richmond Castle. This cave is known as Arthur's Oven; perhaps the name alludes to the legend that King Arthur and his knights sleep in a vast cavern below the keep of Richmond Castle.

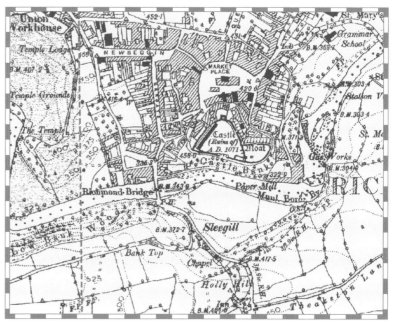

Left: RICHMOND, ARTHUR'S OVEN 1913 65471

Above: RICHMOND, CASTLE WALK 1893 32277

ARTHUR'S OVEN   *Richmond, Yorkshire*

The isolated crag of the Big Stone of Fourstones was of much interest to Victorian antiquaries, for on top of the stone are prehistoric carvings of the type known as cup marks. The Victorians carved the steps into its sides to make access to the summit easier, and generations of graffiti artists have added their initials to the rock, especially to the right of the steps.

THE BIG STONE *Lower Bentham, Yorkshire*

LOWER BENTHAM, THE BIG STONE OF FOURSTONES C1955 L177006

BOROUGHBRIDGE, THE DEVIL'S ARROWS 1895 35295

Raising the devil

One legend associated with this site says that the stones were thrown by the Devil from Howe Hill (near Fountains Abbey) to destroy Aldborough, but as often appears to be the case, the Devil missed his target. Another story says that you can raise the Devil if you walk widdershins (anti-clockwise, or anti-sunwise) around the stones twelve times at midnight.

The Devil's Arrows (35295, left), now three stones, originally four, or perhaps five, stand in North Yorkshire, close to the A1; the site is one of the most famous prehistoric monuments in the county. The stones were brought here from Knaresborough, about six miles away. They range from 18ft to 22ft in height (taller than most of the Stonehenge megaliths), and weigh more than 20 tons each. The unusual deep and curiously fluted grooves are believed to be the result of weathering. They stand in a line running north to south and at intervals of 200ft to 370ft. In Aubrey Burl's paper on the Arrows in the 1991 Yorkshire Archaeological Journal he explains that the Devil's Arrows possess all the features of a classic stone row, in that this alignment leads uphill from water; has a blocking or terminal stone at its lower end; the stones of the row are graded in height with the tallest at the head of the gradient near a stretch of level ground; and the row has an apparent alignment on the most southerly Midsummer rising moon.

THE DEVIL'S ARROWS *Boroughbridge, Yorkshire*

In Roman times, York was the principal military base in Britain – by AD71 the Roman fortress was home to some 6,000 soldiers. The Romans named the outpost Eboracum, which is thought to have meant 'a place of yew trees'. They chose the site because the rivers would help protect it from attack; it is ironic that centuries later the Vikings were to use the rivers as their gateway for invasion. Near the soldiers' encampment a civilian town sprang up – here lived the traders and their families who supplied the soldiers with clothing, food, and much else. One Roman building that still stands is the Multiangular Tower, which stood at the western corner of the Roman fort (the lower part is Roman, but the upper part we see today dates from the 14th century). When this stretch of the city walls was excavated, the archaeologists found that the ramparts dated from Roman, Saxon, Viking, Norman, and medieval times, and that the earth bank grew with each occupation. Other Roman remains visible today include a 30ft column which was found in 1969, lying where it had fallen, during excavations at the Minster. The York Civic Trust had it erected in the Minster Yard in 1971. Also, a public house called the Roman Bath Inn has a floor made up of panels of glass where one can look down on the remains of a Roman bath-house that was excavated in 1930.

Above:
YORK, THE MULTIANGULAR TOWER C1885 18485

The Treasurer's House

In this, one of the most interesting of all the houses in York, a young apprentice plumber stated that while he was working in the cellar, he heard a trumpet playing; then he saw an army of Roman soldiers marching, but as if on their knees. When the cellar floor was dug up, the remains of a Roman road was discovered where the soldiers' feet would have been!

Close by the Minster, it was built in 1419 as a home for the Minster treasurer. It was used for this purpose up until 1547, after which it was sold and had a number of different owners. It is now in the hands of the National Trust.

Left: YORK, THE TREASURER'S HOUSE 1908 59796

YORK, THE VIEW FROM THE CITY WALLS 1897 39492

The Romans built walls spanning nearly three miles in an almost complete circuit around their encampment; chains were stretched across the rivers where they prevented the continuation of the walls. Thus the outpost became a fortress town. Later, the Vikings covered these walls with earth. Then, in medieval times, the walls that still stand today were built on top of the original ramparts with magnesian limestone brought from Tadcaster. The four main entrance gates still survive.

MONASTIC WHITBY

Whitby, Yorkshire

St Hilda came to Whitby in the mid 7th century and founded a monastery whose fame spread far and wide. It was here in AD664 that the Synod of Whitby was held to resolve the differences between Celtic and Roman Christianity, particularly over the date of Easter; following the synod, the English Church was unified under the Roman discipline, and the issue of the date of the Easter festival was settled. Here too dwelt Caedmon, the first English poet. He was an illiterate labourer who worked at the abbey; he was inspired to sing by a vision in which an angel appeared to him, and he told of the creation and God's world in song. When Hilda heard of his talent, she took him into the community and he became a monk, for at this time Whitby was a mixed monastery of both nuns and monks. The early primitive abbey buildings disappeared from the historical record after the mid 8th century, probably destroyed by Viking invaders around AD867. It was not until the 11th century that the stone abbey that is familiar today was begun by Norman Benedictine monks. The abbey was altered and rebuilt over the years. Most of what we see today dates from the 13th and early 14th centuries. Then the greed and rapacity of Henry VIII brought about the end of the monasteries, and the last Abbot of Whitby, Henry de Vall, was forced to surrender the abbey to the king's commissioners in December 1539.

Brother Caedmon, the first English poet, and his song of creation

This cross was erected in 1898 to commemorate Caedmon, the first English poet. Its Celtic design shows the figures of Christ, David, Abbess Hilda and Caedmon. The Venerable Bede, in his 'The Ecclesiastical History of the English Nation' (AD731), tells the story of Caedmon: 'There was in the Monastery of this Abbess a certain brother particularly remarkable for the Grace of God, who was wont to make religious verses, so that whatever was interpreted to him out of scripture, he soon after put the same into poetical expressions of much sweetness and humility in English, which was his native language. By his verse the minds of many were often excited to despise the world, and to aspire to heaven'. Bede also tells how one night Caedmon received a vision in which he was told by an angel to sing of the creation of the world. Bede records the song he sang for the angel, and later sang for Abbess Hilda:

'Praise we the Fashioner now of Heaven's fabric,

The majesty of his might and his mind's wisdom,

Work of the world warden, worker of all wonders,

How he the Lord of Glory everlasting,

Wrought first for the race of men Heaven as a rooftree,

Then made he Middle Earth to be their mansion.'

Opposite page: WHITBY, THE ABBEY 1897
39481

Left: WHITBY, THE CAEDMON CROSS 1901
46783

THE ROMAN RUINS

Ravenglass, Cumbria

Ravenglass was an important naval base for the Romans and was their main supply port for the north of England. A fort, garrisoned by around 1,000 men (of the Cohors I Aelia Classica, a naval unit), was established in AD130 and was known as Glannaventa. The site has suffered from coastal erosion, and the main surviving remnant is the bath-house, now known as Walls Castle, which is one of the largest surviving Roman structures of this kind in England; it measures about 40ft by 90ft, with walls of coursed red stone over 12ft high. Its good state of preservation is thanks to its use as a domestic building into the Middle Ages.

Left: RAVENGLASS, THE ROMAN RUINS C1955 R356030
Below: KENDAL, THE ANCHORITE WELL 2005 K4701K

THE ANCHORITE WELL

Kendal, Cumbria

Kendal's oldest historic site, dating from prehistoric times, is a place now known as the Anchorite Well, situated in the present housing estate of Kirkbarrow which rises above Kirkland. The well is filled by a stream which rises in the fell above and runs down to the river. The well never runs dry, even in the parched summer weather. This quality might have engendered an atmosphere of magic or awe, resulting in a form of worship of the earth or mother goddess. A settlement may have been established in the hollow around the holy well, and this seems to have been the origin of the town. Christianity came to Kendal, either with the Romans or later through Celtic missionaries in the 6th or 7th centuries, and the well became known as the Anchorite Well, named after a hermit who lived nearby; a church was built there, which remained until the Reformation. The well itself suffered dereliction from the 1930s, but has since been restored. It now stands in private land in front of housing, but can be glimpsed through a gate.

THE CASTLERIGG STONE CIRCLE

Keswick, Cumbria

Situated below the Lakeland peaks at the confluence of the Naddle beck and the River Greta, the Castlerigg circle near Keswick has a stunningly beautiful setting; it is one of the oldest stone circles in England (it was constructed in the Neolithic era). It is also still known as the Druids' Circle, although it was erected long before the time of the Druids, who were the priests of the Iron Age Celtic people. The stones are also known as the Keswick Carles. The poet John Keats visited Castlerigg; perhaps he was remembering it when in 'Hyperion' he described the gods as

Druidical Circle near Keswick in Cumberland.

' … *like a dismal cirque*
Of Druid stones, upon a forlorn moor,
When the chill rain begins at shut of eye,
In dull November, and their chancel vault,
The heaven itself, is blinded throughout night.'

The 38 slate stones that form the circle, which is about 100ft across, are graded in height. Two large stones are to the north, where the entrance is, and from there to the south-east the stones increase in size. To the east there is an outlying stone, over which the sun rises at the spring and autumn equinox. To the south-west is another stone in the direction of the midwinter sunset, which is a far more useful calendar date for ancient agricultural communities. Three stone axes were found in or near the circle in the 19th century; the circle is situated near a Neolithic axe 'factory'.

At the northern end of the circle, the two larger stones form an entrance; inside, on the eastern side of the circle, are the remains of ten stones arranged in an oblong, whose purpose is unknown. In 1725, the antiquary William Stukely recorded a second circle to the west, but nothing remains of this.

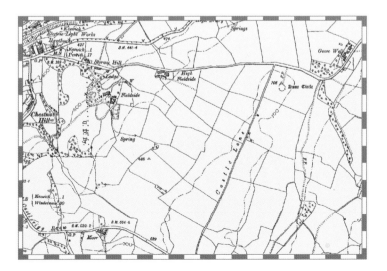

Top: KESWICK, THE CASTLERIGG STONE CIRCLE 1895 36951

THE GIANT'S GRAVE AND THUMB

Penrith, Cumbria

The Giant's Grave in St Andrew's churchyard at Penrith is actually a collection of two badly weathered 10th-century cross shafts and four Norse 'hogback' tombstones (32926, left). Stories about the grave have been linked not only with the mythical giant Sir Owen Caesarius and the Arthurian legends, but also with Owain, son of Urien, a 6th-century King of Rheged, and Owen, King of Cumbria from AD920-937.

The Giant's Thumb (32927, above) stands close to the Giant's Grave and is another badly eroded stone cross dating to about AD920. The carvings on both the Giant's Thumb and the Giant's Grave show an intriguing mixture of Anglian, Celtic and Norse decorative motifs, indicating that in the 10th century the area around Penrith must have been something of a cultural melting pot. In later years, the Giant's Thumb was used as a public pillory.

Left: PENRITH, THE GIANT'S GRAVE 1893 32926

Above: PENRITH, THE GIANT'S THUMB 1893 32927

MAYBURGH HENGE

Eamont Bridge, Cumbria

Just south of Penrith, near the River Eamont, Mayburgh Henge is a massive circular bank constructed from water-worn stones, about 4.5m high, enclosing an area about 90m in diameter. The single stone at the centre, nearly 3m high, is thought to be the last remaining stone of a setting of four recorded in a drawing of the henge made in 1664. The henge was built in the Neolithic era, and is one of a group of three prehistoric monuments near Eamont Bridge, known collectively as the Penrith Henges; the other two are King Arthur's Round Table (another henge) and the Little Round Table, although little remains of the latter. From inside the single eastern entrance to Mayburgh Henge there is a view towards King Arthur's Round Table, and there used to be a pair of stones just outside the entrance.

Left: EAMONT BRIDGE,
MAYBURGH HENGE
1893 32935P

THE SAXON CHURCH

Escomb, County Durham

The small 7th-century church of St John the Evangelist is one of the finest examples of early Christian architecture in the north. Built largely from stone salvaged from the abandoned Roman fort at Binchester, St John's lay semi-derelict in the 1870s; it might well have been allowed to fall into complete ruin, had it not been for the Reverend R E Hooppell, who recognised St John's importance and launched an appeal to save it. The long nave and narrow chancel are typical of Northumbrian ecclesiastical architecture. Later additions include a 12th-century porch and 13th- and 19th-century windows.

Left: ESCOMB, THE SAXON CHURCH 1898 41463

The chancel of Jarrow's St Paul's Church dates from the 7th century; it was once the church of the Venerable Bede's monastery, and inside is a stone slab inscribed with an inscription recording the dedication of the church on 23 April AD685. The tower was built in the late 11th century. Close by are the remains of the Benedictine monastery which was built on the site of the important Anglo-Saxon monastery where the Venerable Bede lived and worked (AD673–735). Bede is famous for being the first English historian, and his work 'The Ecclesiastical History of the English People' is valuable source material for historians of this period. Bede was also responsible for devising the AD and BC dating system for dates before and after the birth of Christ.

Right: JARROW, ST PAUL'S CHURCH C1965 J5015

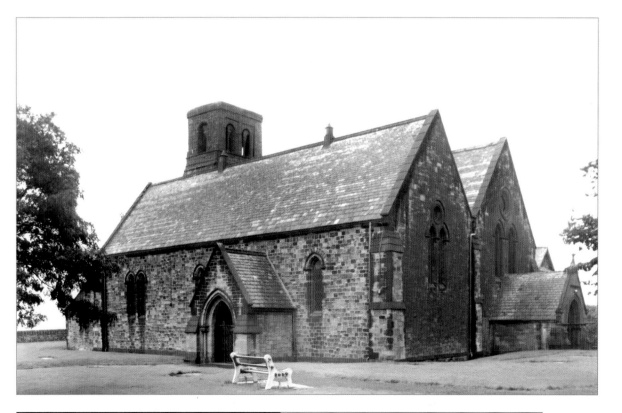

| BEDE'S CHURCH | *Jarrow, Northumberland* |

193

HADRIAN'S WALL

Northumberland

The impressive ruins shown in C459012 (left) are of a Roman fort that was built in the time of the Roman governor Agricola in about AD80 to guard an important crossing on the River Tyne. It stood on the main road north from York, and was used during the Agricolan period as a base during campaigns in the north. It was later used as a very important military supply depot for Hadrian's Wall. To the right, in the distance, we can just see the seven-arched bridge of 1674 spanning the Tyne.

The cavalry fort at Chesters, about a mile from Chollerford, was called Cilurnum by the Romans. It is exceptionally well preserved, as we can see from the photographs. Photograph 76659 (below left) shows the large entrance hall and dressing room of the bath-house; the niches in the wall may have contained statues, or they may simply have been where the soldiers left their clothes and belongings. From this room a door led to the latrines, which were flushed by the waste water from the baths. Another door led to a lobby giving onto the various rooms of the baths, including a tepidarium or warm room, heated by a hypocaust, and a caldarium, or hot room, where a large boiler heated water for the hot bath in an apsidal bay in the caldarium (76658, right). Other rooms included a sweating chamber (sudatorium), an intensely hot room (laconicum), and a cold room with a cold plunge bath.

Above left: CORBRIDGE, CORSTOPITUM C1955 C459012

Below left: CHOLLERFORD, CHESTERS (CILURNUM), RECESSES IN THE BATH-HOUSE 1924 76659

CHOLLERFORD, CHESTERS (CILURNUM), THE HYPOCAUST OF THE BATH-HOUSE 1924 76658

Cilurnum was part of the Hadrian's Wall defences; it was built soon after the Wall was completed in about AD122. It was garrisoned by various forces over a period of about 300 years. It is the standard playing-card shape of Roman military forts, and it was built astride the Wall, with three of the main gateways, the north, east and west gates, opening on the north side of the Wall. It is the best-preserved Roman cavalry fort in Britain: the visible remains include the gateways, the ornate headquarters building (with its courtyard, hall, regimental chapel and strongroom), and the commanding officer's house, as well as two barrack blocks and the military bath-house. The remains of a Roman bridge over the North Tyne can also be found in the area.

The exterior of St Giles's Church at Chollerton is mainly 18th- and 19th-century, but the interior tells a different story: this is 12th-century, and consists of an arcade of four bays (C456009, above). The monolithic Roman columns possibly came from Chesters. A Roman altar dedicated to Jupiter was found buried in the churchyard in the early 19th century; it was inverted and used as one of the fonts.

A Roman Legionary tells us about the Wall

'Along the top are towers with guard-houses, small towers, between. Even on the narrowest part of it three men with shields can walk abreast, from guard-house to guardhouse. A little curtain wall, no higher than a man's neck, runs along the top of the thick wall, so that from a distance you see the helmets of the sentries sliding back and forth like beads. Thirty feet high is the Wall, and on the Picts' side, the North, is a ditch, strewn with blades of old swords and spear-heads set in wood, and tyres of wheels joined by chains.'

RUDYARD KIPLING, 'PUCK OF POOK'S HILL' (1906)

The Murder House

Outside the fort at Housesteads was a civilian settlement, much of which has yet to be excavated. However, one house, excavated in 1932, is known as the Murder House because of the mysterious skeletons of a man and a woman which were discovered beneath the floor. Part of a sword was found between the man's ribs, and since burial within a settlement was forbidden by Roman law, it was assumed that the couple were murdered and their bodies secretly hidden.

The line of Hadrian's Wall on either side of the fort of Housesteads is one of the best-preserved sections to be seen (76655, opposite above right, and 76657, above right). The Roman name of the fort was formerly thought to be Borcovicium, or Borcovicus, but a dedicatory inscription found on the actual site suggests that it may in fact have been Vercovicium. It guarded a gap in the ridge (the Whin Sill), the course of the Knag Burn, which also gave the fort proximity to a good water supply. The fort was refurbished around AD200, after which it was garrisoned by an auxiliary infantry cohort, the Cohors I Tungrorum, from the Roman province of Belgica, roughly the modern-day Belgium. It is one of the most complete Roman forts in Britain; here the visitor can see the remains of the four gates, the military headquarters, the commandant's house, barrack blocks, granaries, a hospital (a unique survival), and latrines.

Left: HOUSESTEADS, THE ROMAN FORT 1924 76654

Above: HOUSESTEADS, HADRIAN'S WALL 1924 76657

Near Bardon Mill (76665, above) is the highest point of Hadrian's Wall, at 345m above sea level. The Roman fort of Vindolanda stands between here and Once Brewed. The lookout and signalling post on the crest of Winshields Crags commanded a vast uninterrupted view, but it would have been extremely windy.

I have sent you ... pairs of socks, two pairs of sandals and two pairs of underpants ...

In 1973, fragments of 1,500 wooden tablets were found at Vindolanda (the total has since risen to almost 2,000). The fragments were found to be an assortment of letters, administrative records, and other trivia – even an invitation to a birthday party from the wife of one commanding officer to another: 'Claudia Severa to her Lepidina, greetings. On the third day before the Ides of September, sister, for the day of the celebration of my birthday, I give you a warm invitation to make sure that you come to us, to make the day more enjoyable for me by your arrival, if you are present. Give my greetings to your Cerialis. My Aelius and my little son send him their greetings. I shall expect you, sister. Farewell, sister, my dearest soul, as I hope to prosper, and hail.' This was written by Claudia Severa, wife of Brocchus (commander of an unidentified fort called Briga) to Sulpicia Lepidina, wife of Flavius Cerialis. Cerialis was the praefectus in command of Cohors IX Batavorum, which occupied Vindolanda from around AD97 onwards. The tablets are full of the small details of everyday service on the Wall, and provide a fascinating insight to the lives of those lonely men on their windswept hills, which must have seemed like a posting to the end of the known world. One mother wrote to her soldier son: 'I have sent you ... pairs of socks, two pairs of sandals and two pairs of underpants.'

The section shown in 76661 (opposite left) is a narrow part of the Wall, since orders were received in AD125 to reduce its width. Hadrian's Wall stretched from Wallsend to Bowness, a distance of 73 miles. Each section of Hadrian's Wall contains a plaque engraved with the details of the unit that built it and the centurion in charge of construction. Hadrian's Wall was designated a World Heritage Site in 1987, making it one of 721 world treasures alongside the Taj Mahal, the Great Wall of China and Stonehenge.

Hadrian's Wall was painstakingly built out of stone and turf by the Romans around AD120. It was created to span the entire width of Britain and so prevent military invasions from the north by the Pictish tribes of Scotland. It also succeeded in stabilising the regional economy and encouraging peace among the various factions. It clearly defined the physical frontier that separated the savage Selgovae tribe in the north from the Brigantes in the south. This was a clever move by the Romans, for it discouraged the tribes from forming a single united force. The Wall was the northern border of the Roman Empire in Britain for hundreds of years, and was certainly the most heavily defended fortification in the Roman Empire. Trade and commerce, of course, had to go on, and there were gates through the wall with customs posts so that merchandise could be authorised and taxed accordingly.

This central part of Hadrian's Wall (76662, left) contains some of the best-preserved sections; here the wall strides along the edge of Whin Sill escarpment, from which there are spectacular views.

Opposite left: GILSLAND, HADRIAN'S WALL 1924 76661

Opposite right: BARDON MILL, THE ROMAN MILESTONE NEAR VINDOLANDA 1924 76665

Left: GILSLAND, THE ROMAN WALL, CRAG LOUGH 1924 76662

GILSLAND, ROMAN ALTARS AND STONES 1924 76660

Along Hadrian's Wall can be found many carvings and engravings left by the legionaries and their followers whilst they were stationed on the Wall. Some of the carvings are altars to the gods – some to Roman gods, like Mars, god of war, and the goddess Fortuna; some to Mithras, originally a god from the Far East; and some to Celtic gods. Were these Roman altars and inscribed stones picked up over the years and used to make a garden wall? Where are these stones today? Let us hope that they are in the care of a museum.

Birdoswald (76664, left) was the Roman fort of Camboglanna, which means 'crooked glen' – the fort overlooks the twisting gorge of the River Irthing, and was built to guard the bridge at Willowford. Covering an area of about four acres, the fort contained granaries, a large basilica-shaped drill hall, a hospital, barrack blocks, the commandant's house and the headquarters building. Outside the protective curtain walls was the parade ground, as well as the graveyard and a small civilian settlement. The fort was first occupied by a cavalry regiment, and later in the 3rd century by Cohors I Aelia Dacorum Millaria, an infantry regiment from the Lower Danube, today's Romania. The buildings were taken over by local people for storage and defensive purposes long after the Romans left Britain, including the west gatehouse, which was still standing and being used by local farmers in the 16th century. Today the walls still stand to a good height, but no buildings remain inside.

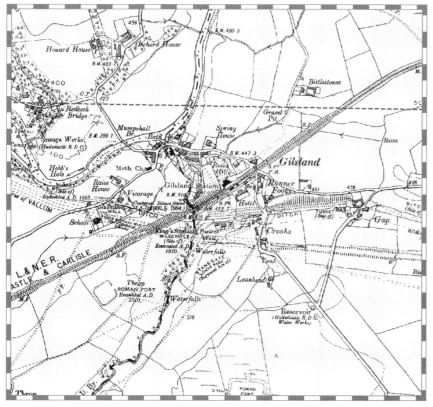

Above left: GILSLAND, BIRDOSWALD, THE EAST GATE 1924 76664

Right: GILSLAND, THE CROSS, BEWCASTLE 1924 76663

ANGLIAN CROSS

Gilsland, Northumberland

This 7th-century cross stands 4.4m tall, and is thought to have been carved for the Anglian King Alcfrith. It has wonderful carvings of biblical figures on one side, and animals, trees, fruit and birds decorate the others.

THE CASTLE — *Bamburgh, Northumberland*

This has been a fortified site since the 6th century, when it was the residence of the Northumbrian kings. King Oswald was the first Christian king to live here, and was so admired and respected by St Aidan of Lindisfarne that Aidan once grasped the king's hand, saying: 'Never let this hand consume or wither'. When Oswald was later killed in battle, his hand was cut off and revered as a sacred relic in Bamburgh church, apparently remaining uncorrupted. The Norman keep with its four corner turrets, similar to that at Rochester, was built between 1164 and 1170, and was besieged by William II (William Rufus) in 1095. Unable to take the fortress from Robert de Mowbray, 3rd Earl of Northumberland, William headed south, leaving the prosecution of the siege to others. Mowbray attempted to escape, but was captured. His wife only surrendered Bamburgh after her husband had been paraded before the walls under threat of having his eyes torn out. Following an eventful history, the medieval buildings of Bamburgh Castle were in ruins when they were sold to the Bishop of Durham, Lord Crewe, in 1704. In 1757 a trustee of the Crewe estate began restorations. The castle was further restored in the late 19th and early 20th centuries.

Above: BAMBURGH, THE CASTLE C1960 B547029

The Laidley Worm

An old story associated with Bamburgh Castle is that of the Laidley Worm. Long ago one of the Northumbrian kings at Bamburgh remarried, not knowing that his new wife was a witch. She was jealous of the king's daughter, and turned her into a dragon, or 'worm'. This dragon ravaged the surrounding countryside and terrified the inhabitants. The king's son, the Childe of Wynde, who was overseas, heard of the dragon and returned home to kill the monster and restore peace to his father's kingdom. The Childe approached the dragon with drawn sword, not knowing that the monster was actually his sister. But even through her enchantment the princess recognised her brother. The voice of the girl came through the dragon's jaws, saying:

'O, quit your sword, unbend your bow,
And give me kisses three;
For though I am a poisonous worm,
No harm I'll do to thee.

O, quit your sword, unbend your bow,
And give me kisses three;
If I'm not won ere set of sun,
Won never shall I be.'

Recognising his sister's voice, the young man bravely kissed the dragon three times. The spell was broken, and the princess explained how the spell had come about. The Childe entered the castle, where he found the wicked queen cowering in her bower. The Childe struck her with a twig of the magical rowan tree, and turned her into an ugly toad. The toad hopped away, and is said to live still in a cave below the castle.

ST CUTHBERT'S CHAPEL

Farne Islands, Northumberland

According to Bede, St Aidan retired to Inner Farne for solitude, and later St Cuthbert also came here, dying on Farne Island in AD687. A Benedictine cell from Durham was established here in 1246, and a chapel dedicated to St Cuthbert was built in 1370. After buying the islands in the 19th century, Archdeacon Thorp set about a heavy restoration of the chapel, which included second-hand panelling and pews from Durham Cathedral.

LINDISFARNE PRIORY

Holy Island, Northumberland

HOLY ISLAND, LINDISFARNE PRIORY C1940 H348012

The name 'Lindisfarne' was given to this island by the first Anglo-Saxons to live here, and it became known as 'Holy Island' later, reflecting its importance in the religious history of Britain. The first monastery was built around AD635 when St Aidan and his monks came here from Iona, and the exceedingly holy St Cuthbert was ordained Bishop of Lindisfarne in AD685. Ill health soon forced Cuthbert to resign his see, and he died on Farne Island in AD687. He was buried at Lindisfarne and his tomb soon became a place of pilgrimage. So many miracles were reported at his grave that Cuthbert was called 'the Wonder-Worker of England', and he was canonised eleven years after his death. The island was then devastated by a Viking attack in AD793 and the monks fled with the precious relics of St Cuthbert, which eventually found a new resting place in Durham. After the Norman Conquest the Benedictine monks of Durham built another monastery to continue St Cuthbert's association with Lindisfarne, and the ruins of this building can be seen today - the first, wooden, monastery of St Aidan has disappeared, but the present church of St Mary the Virgin probably stands on its site.

The Vikings came from Norway, Sweden, and Denmark; their name comes from their term 'to go a-viking', or to embark on raids. They were superb seamen and navigators, and their shallow-draught ships could sail up rivers from the coast, allowing them to reach deep into the countryside and raid rich inland sites such as religious houses. Fear of the Vikings dominated Europe from the 8th to the 11th centuries. In AD793 Lindisfarne, one of Britain's most sacred sites, was sacked by Viking raiders. The Christian world recoiled in horror, and Alcuin of York wrote to Ethelred, King of Northumbria: 'Lo, it is nearly 350 years that we and our fathers have inhabited this most lovely land, and never before has such terror appeared in Britain as we have now suffered from a pagan race, nor was it thought that such an inroad from the sea could be made. Behold the church of St Cuthbert spattered with the blood of the priests of God, despoiled of all its ornaments; a place more venerable than all in Britain is given as a prey to pagan peoples.' In later years the Vikings themselves became settlers and colonised much of northern England, with a major settlement at York, or 'Jorvik'. They founded Dublin in AD836, and established settlements in Iceland, the Isle of Man, the Orkney and Shetland Islands, and Greenland. They are also believed to have reached the coast of America. Viking warriors formed part of the Emperor's bodyguard at Byzantium, and developed trade routes into Russia. One of their few endearing habits were the colourful names that they went in for, such as Eric Bloodaxe, Harold Bluetooth, Ivar the Boneless, Sweyn Forkbeard, and Sigurdsson Hairy Britches.

Right: HOLY ISLAND, LINDISFARNE PRIORY, THE ANCIENT DOORWAY 1950 H348119

Above: HOLY ISLAND, ST AIDAN'S STATUE C1960 H348169

The period of Aidan's first monastery is known as the 'Golden Age' of Lindisfarne. With the permission and support of King Oswald (of Bamburgh), Aidan and his monks worked as missionaries among the pagan English of Northumbria. The monks set up schools to teach reading, writing, and the study of Christian texts, and trained missionaries to spread the Gospel all over Anglo-Saxon England. Lindisfarne is often seen as the cradle of English Christianity. The monastery became known for the beauty of the illuminated manuscripts that were produced there, of which the Lindisfarne Gospels, currently in the care of the British Library, is a superb example.

By AD75 the Romans were able to build their large legionary fortress at Caerleon, in South Wales. They called it Isca, probably after the River Usk. The legion based at Isca was the Second Augustan Legion, named after the Emperor Augustus, which was one of the four legions that took part in the original invasion of Britain in AD43. A legion was a force of about 5,500 men, and the Second Augustan's name is seen on many inscriptions found in the area.

The most impressive of the Roman remains at Caerleon is the amphitheatre. Built in about AD90, just outside the fortress walls, it is the only fully excavated amphitheatre to be seen in Britain (the work was carried out by Mortimer Wheeler and his wife Tessa in 1926 and 1927). It could seat around 6,000 people, so it would have been able to accommodate the whole legion if necessary. An amphitheatre was primarily meant for entertainment, and would have been the venue for gladiatorial contests as well as games and military training. There may also have been wild animal fights, though probably not with exotic animals such as lions and tigers. More likely, for a fortress and town on the edge of the Empire, the Romans would have used animals then found in the local area: wolves, bears, wild boars and cattle.

The amphitheatre was built of stone and would have had a wooden superstructure to take the seating. The arena was oval and was about 56m long by 41m broad. There were eight entrances into the arena, two main processional entrances at either end, and six smaller entrances with direct access to the seating area. This would enable soldiers watching events in the amphitheatre to have easy access to the arena to participate in any activities. Of particular interest is a small room blocking the eastern side-entrance. This has stone seats and a brick niche where a statue or altar could have been placed. It has been identified as a waiting room where gladiators or other contestants remained until it was their turn to enter the arena.

On early maps of Caerleon the amphitheatre field is known as the Round Table Field, and there are strong literary connections between Caerleon and the legends of King Arthur. It is certainly a possibility that it was a meeting place for a post-Roman military ruler and his army; and, unlike the famous wooden Round Table at Winchester, the amphitheatre would have been in existence in what is now generally recognised as being the 'historical' King Arthur's time.

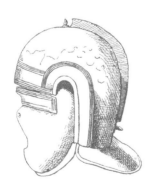

Top: CAERLEON, THE ROMAN AMPHITHEATRE 1954 C4030

Right: CAERLEON, THE AMPHITHEATRE, A ROMAN MILITARY RE-ENACTMENT 2003 N25716K

CRUG DIAL

Abergavenny, Gwent

Crug Dial, the Stone of Revenge, stands on the ridge between the Grwyne Fawr and Llanthony valleys, to the north of the hill-fort of Twyn-y-Gaer. It commemorates a bloody encounter in April 1136. Richard de Clare, a member of one of the most powerful Norman families in Wales, was returning from a visit to Abergavenny Castle when he was ambushed and killed by a band of Welshmen led by Iorwerth ap Owain of Caerleon, grandson of the last Welsh King of Gwent. As he approached the Black Mountains, de Clare had foolishly dismissed the escort he had been given by the Lord of Abergavenny, Brian de Wallingford. Then, in the dark wooded valley of Grwyne Fawr, he and his party were slain.

ABERGAVENNY, CRUG DIAL, THE STONE OF REVENGE 2005 A9703K

HAROLD'S STONES | *Trelleck, Gwent*

These prehistoric standing stones give Trelleck its name, which is thought to derive from the old Welsh for 'three stones'. Their original purpose is unknown; it is possible that they were designed to align with the Skirrid Mountain, sometimes called 'Holy Mountain of Gwent', at the winter solstice. They may possibly have once been part of a larger monument such as a stone circle. Their name reflects a tradition that they were built to commemorate a battle won by King Harold, but they are much older, and are more likely to date from the Bronze Age. Local legend tells that they were thrown by a giant called Jack o' Kent when he was playing at pitch and toss with the Devil.

Above: TRELLECK, HAROLD'S STONES 2004 T266701K

THE WELLS

Clydach, Gwent

The old name for this spot at the foot of the Clydach Vale was Cwm Pwca (Puck's Valley). Local legend has it that Shakespeare heard stories of Welsh fairies from his friend Richard Price, son of Sir John Price of the Priory, Brecon, and based 'A Midsummer Night's Dream' on what he was told; this legend was certainly known to the poet Campbell, who wrote in 1833: 'I discovered a probability – almost near a certainty – that Shakespeare visited friends in the very town (Brecon in Wales) where Mrs Siddons [the actress] was born, and that he there found in a neighbouring glen, called 'The Valley of Fairy Puck', the principal machinery of his 'Midsummer Night's Dream'.'

THE DRUID STONES *Pontypridd, Mid-Glamorgan*

The stone circle and spiral around the Rocking Stone are relatively modern: stone circles are still being erected in Wales, and are known as Gorsedd Stones. They are raised when the local town hosts the National Eisteddfod, an annual arts festival of poetry and singing. However, it is possible that the Rocking Stone itself was left in its position by glacial action, and some traditions are associated with it. It can be rocked by pressure on the eastern part of the top slab, and at one time it was said that the rock would vibrate at the touch of a child.

Previous page:
PONTYPRIDD, THE DRUID STONES 1899 43622

Left:
PONTYPRIDD, THE ROCKING STONE 1899 43620

A hillside enigma – the Eisteddfod circle

The extensive circle of stones seen in photograph 43622 (previous page) above the town of Pontypridd is not as ancient as it may appear. It was conceived and built in 1850 by a local antiquary, Evan Davis, for his initiation as Arch Druid of the revived National Eisteddfod. The two fine concentric circles enclose the Rocking Stone, which is a genuine glacial erratic. The Eisteddfod has ancient origins going back to the 12th century, but a national event had not been held since the Elizabethan era. Then in the 1790s the old ceremony of the National Eisteddfod was revived. Sixty years later, Evan Davis, fired with enthusiasm by the antiquarian William Stukeley and his theories about Druidism, built this circle on the hill above Pontypridd, based on the Avebury configuration. The circle was used for ceremonial processions and Bardic ritual three or four times a year up until the 1920s. Evan Davis set into motion a custom of constructing a new stone circle for each successive National Eisteddfod, and examples can be found in many Welsh locations, including Cardiff and Mountain Ash. In the foreground of the picture are the sacred Bardic signs, carved in stone and wood.

KING ARTHUR'S STONE
Reynoldston, West Glamorgan

The area of Cefn Bryn, the backbone of the Gower peninsula, is scattered with around 70 Neolithic tombs, the most famous of which is Arthur's Stone, or Maen Ceti in Welsh. In ancient Welsh texts King Arthur's Stone was named as one of the 'Three Wonderful Things of Britain', along with Stonehenge and Silbury Hill. The vast 25-ton capstone was deposited here during the last Ice Age, and at one time was even larger, but a section has broken off.

Many legends have developed around King Arthur's Stone. One of them is that the capstone was a pebble in King Arthur's boot which he threw away, and it landed on Cefn Bryn. King Arthur himself is said to ride a white horse near the stone on moonlit nights, and the stone is also believed to go down to the sea for a drink on Old Year's Night (New Year's Eve).

Left:
REYNOLDSTON, KING ARTHUR'S STONE
1893   32761

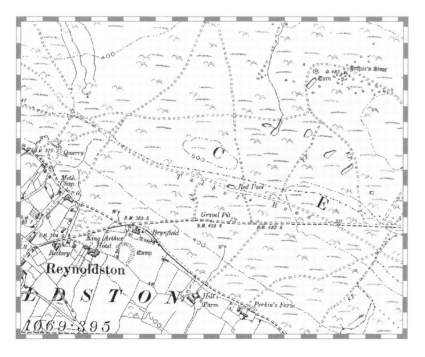

THE THREE FACES
Llandaff, South Glamorgan

In the 6th century St Dyfrig founded the renowned cathedral at Llandaff, close to the River Taff. He was succeeded by St Teilo and then by Teilo's nephew, Euddogwy. These three Celtic saints remain the patron saints of the present cathedral, and are represented by the carving known as the three faces and four eyes.

Right:
LLANDAFF, THE CATHEDRAL,
A CAPITAL — THREE FACES AND
FOUR EYES C1955 L67046

THE CELTIC CROSS — *Carew, Dyfed*

This intricately carved Celtic cross dates from the 11th century and stands about 13ft high. There are well-preserved panels of knotwork and key patterns on its east and west faces, and an inscription on the west face of the cross commemorates Maredudd ap Edwin, joint ruler of the kingdom of Deheubarth in south-west Wales, who died two years into his reign in 1035.

Above: CAREW, THE CELTIC CROSS
C1960 C24009

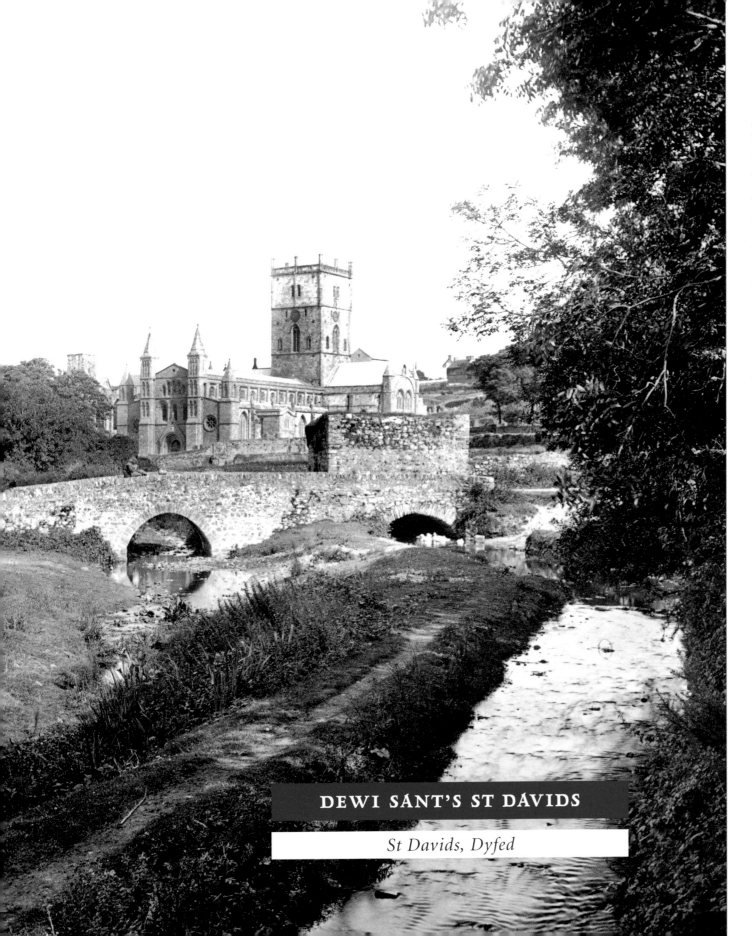

St Davids, or Tyddewi, is named after Dewi Sant, the patron saint of Wales (he died on 1 March AD588), who established his monastery here on the banks of the River Alun. The tiny city also boasts the remains of the impressive Bishop's Palace. The legend has it that David, about to speak to an assembled crowd, was concerned that they would not be able to see him. He dropped his handkerchief onto the ground, which sank down, forming a hollow, a natural amphitheatre in which everyone could take in what he was saying – the cathedral was built on this spot. However, it is more likely that the cathedral was built in a hollow to hide it from the marauding Danes. The complex, much of which can still be seen today, was once surrounded by a curtain wall – the Norman response to its having been attacked and pillaged at least eight times.

THE BISHOP'S PALACE

DEWI SANT'S ST DAVIDS

St Davids, Dyfed

Left: ST DAVIDS CATHEDRAL FROM THE SOUTH-WEST 1890 27908

St Davids is in a somewhat austere location on its windswept plateau, but the interior of the cathedral is simply stunning (27915, above). The roof beams were renewed in the 19th century. The bishop's throne, dating from c1500, is on the right in front of the open wooden screen which separates the choir from the presbytery. The tomb beyond the screen is that of Edmund Tudor, Earl of Richmond, the father of Henry VII, the first Tudor monarch.

St Mary's Chapel (27920, right) is located in the ruins of the extensive Bishop's Palace, which is now much restored. William the Conqueror once journeyed here to pray in this well-known place of pilgrimage – two pilgrimages to St David's was considered equal to a pilgrimage to Rome.

Above: ST DAVIDS CATHEDRAL, THE CHOIR, LOOKING EAST 1890 27915

Right: ST DAVIDS, THE CATHEDRAL CLOSE, ST MARY'S CHAPEL 1890 27920

ST GOVÁN'S CHÁPEL — *Tenby, Dyfed*

ST GOVAN'S HEAD, THE CHAPEL AND THE STEPS 18903 24928

The present chapel was built in the 13th century and contains an altar, a bench and a cell hewn out of rock. It is thought that the original chapel or hermitage dates from the 5th century. Legends as to its origin abound. One has it that it was the retreat of Cofen, wife of a king of Glamorgan; another that this is where Sir Gawaine became a hermit after King Arthur's death. A third is as follows: 'Here, according to a curious old legend, St Govan sought shelter from his pagan enemies; whereupon the massy rock closed over him and hid him from his pursuers, opening again to release the pious anchorite as soon as the chase was overpassed.' (H Thornhill Timmins, 1895.)

215

TWO ENIGMAS

Llanbedr, Gwynedd

Although a tradition says that the steps shown in 1758b (left) date from Roman times, they are more likely to have their origins in the medieval period as part of a packhorse trail for transporting wool from the Bala area to the seaport of Pensarn.

Near Llanbedr, about three miles from Dyffryn in Wales, are two standing stones, one over 10ft high (30212, right). The stones are now enclosed with railings, and their original purpose remains a mystery. Could they have been part of a stone circle?

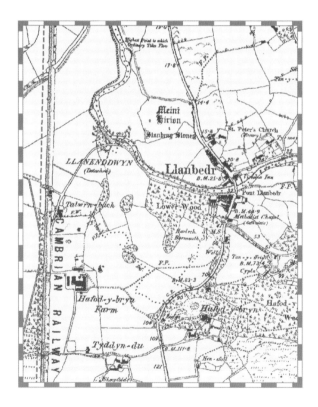

Left: LLANBEDR, THE ROMAN STEPS C1863 1758B

Right: LLANBEDR, TWO LONG STONES 1892 30212

BEDDGELERT, GELERT'S GRAVE C1900 B49301

This magnificent view (84742, right) shows Beddgelert cupped in an encircling ring of mountains. It was described in the late 1890s as 'nestling in a deep romantic vale, engirt by lofty mountains, amidst the grandest scenery in Wales'. It is the perfect site for the ancient priory that once stood here; it was attached to the house of St Celert, and pilgrims have made their way here for centuries. The small stone village of Beddgelert is the supposed burial place of Prince Llewelyn's beloved dog Gelert (see below). Yet until about 1800, the village was known as Beddcelert, the grave of St Celert.

The tragic death of faithful Gelert

The story goes that Prince Llewelyn returned home to be greeted by his favourite dog, Gelert, with his muzzle covered in blood. Thinking that the dog had killed his baby son, the prince drew his sword and slew him. He then found his baby alive, lying next to the body of a wolf. The heartbroken prince then realised that in fact Gelert had saved the baby by defending him from the attack of the wolf.

BEDDGELERT, THE VIEW TOWARDS
SNOWDON 1931   84742

This double-chambered Neolithic portal tomb is most unusual, in that its minor chamber butts up against the larger one, instead of being separated from it by a few metres as is usually the case. The monument stands within Lord Anglesey's Plas Newydd estate; it stands in a magnificent position overlooking the Menai Straits, where 'it at once suggests an 18th-century folly, an ornament to the house put up by some romantically minded peer.' (Jacquetta Hawkes, 'The Prehistoric and Roman Monuments in England and Wales', 1951.)

Above: MENAI,
THE PLAS
NEWYDD
CROMLECH
1890   23206

The caves at Cefn are amongst a number in the Elwy Valley; they were already famous in the 1530s, when John Leland mentioned them in his famous Itinerary of 1536–39. Both animal and human remains were found in Cefn Old Cave and Cefn New Cave between the 1830s and 1870s. In a cave nearby, at Pontnewydd, excavations between the 1970s and 1990s found stone tools and animal and human bones from the Neanderthal period. These date from about a quarter of a million years ago, some of the earliest remains found in Britain. It is probable that these caves were originally much deeper than they are today – weathering of the rock has made the entrances further back than they were.

St Mary's Well (23305, above) can be found at the bottom of a steep flight of steps leading towards the river. It is said that the well has pre-Christian origins and its waters were considered a cure for a number of disorders. In later centuries the well was used as a source of water for domestic purposes, but it had fallen into disuse by the early 20th century. In 1990 it was restored, and placed within an enclosed walled garden.

Top: ST ASAPH, THE CEFN CAVES 1890 23303

Above: ST ASAPH, ST MARY'S WELL 1890 23305

Right: ST ASAPH, THE STEPS TO THE CEFN CAVES 1891 29184

Opposite: ST ASAPH, THE CEFN CAVES C1875 506GP

ST WINEFRIDE'S WELL *Holywell, Clywd*

HOLYWELL, THE BATH, ST WINEFRIDE'S WELL C1930 H522001

Dating from the 7th century, and named after Winefride, or Gwenffrewi in Welsh, this holy well has been the site of pilgrimage ever since, and is known as 'the Lourdes of Wales'. The waters are said to have amazing restorative powers, and Henry V came here to pray in 1415 before the Battle of Agincourt. The visitors here are probably not pilgrims, but merely appreciating one of the 'Seven Wonders of Wales'.

TRIMONTIUM *Newstead, Borders*

This monument, in the style of a Roman altar, was unveiled in 1928. The inscription reads: 'Here once stood the fort of Trimontium, built by the troops of Agricola in the first century AD, abandoned at least twice by the Romans, and ultimately lost by them after fully one hundred years of frontier warfare.' The fields behind the monument once contained a very large Roman fort named Trimontium, or 'the place of three hills', which commanded the Tweed valley and was a key defensive site. Excavations of the site have revealed many pits, or wells, which contained either rubbish or votive offerings, such as helmets, tools and animal heads.

One of the most intriguing finds at Trimontium was the almost complete skeleton of a dwarf, whose age was estimated as being about 23 years old, and whose height was about 4ft 6 inches. There was no sign of bone disease or rickets, but the remains suggested a slight, slender build. The skeleton was found buried beneath the bodies of nine horses. No explanation can be offered.

GRANNY KEMPOCK

Gourock, Strathclyde

Above: GOUROCK, GRANNY KEMPOCK 1900   45983

This prehistoric standing stone stands on the hill above Kempock Point, overlooking the firth. It is known as 'Granny Kempock' because of its resemblance to a hooded old woman. It was regarded as lucky by sailors and fishermen, who tried to ensure good luck for fair winds and a safe journey before setting out to sea by circling the stones seven times, carrying a basket of sand and chanting a 'weird song'. In 1662 a young girl named Mary Lamont was burned to death as a witch after confessing that she had planned to throw the stone into the sea to cause shipwrecks. It was also the custom for newly-wed couples to walk around the stone seven times to make their marriages happy, lucky and fruitful. This custom has obvious fertility rite origins, which may be explained by an alternative theory that, far from looking like an old woman, the stone bears more resemblance to a phallic symbol.

INCHCOLM ABBEY

Inchcolm, Fife

The ruins of Inchcolm Abbey, 'the Iona of the East', are amongst the best preserved monastic buildings in Scotland, fulfilling the wish on a medieval Latin inscription above one of the abbey doorways: 'Stet domus haec donec fluctus formica marinos ebibat, et totum testudo perambulet orbem' – 'May this house stand until an ant drains the flowing sea, and a tortoise walks around the whole world'. Inchcolm is a tiny island in the Firth of Forth just off the coast of Fife. Here in 1123 Alexander I took refuge – he was crossing the Forth when a storm came up – and was tended by a hermit, whose ancient cell still stands close to the abbey. In gratitude, the king vowed to found an abbey dedicated to St Columba; however, his death the following year meant that the abbey was built by his successor David I. The abbey as we see it today was built at different times, with the abbey church itself the oldest part.

There is a tradition that following the defeat of the Danes by Macbeth at the 11th-century Battle of Kinghorn, the Danes paid in gold for the right to have their dead buried on the island of Inchcolm. Shakespeare must have been aware of this story, for it is mentioned in 'Macbeth':

'Sweno, the Norways' king, craves composition:
Nor would we deign him burial of his men
Till he disbursed at Saint Colme's inch
Ten thousand dollars to our general use.'

FOWLIS WESTER, THE CROSS C1950 F1183002

THE CROSS

Fowlis Wester, Tayside

The small village of Fowlis Wester is in an area rich in ancient sites. This Pictish cross slab has now been removed to the village church for safekeeping, and a replica stands in its place. The meaning and relevance of the carvings on this cross have now been lost to us, but they show two horsemen and various symbols on one side, and a man leading a cow with a bell, followed by six other men, on the other. The village church is dedicated to St Bean, who died cAD720. He was the grandson of the King of Leinster, in Ireland, and was famous for preaching to the Picts in this area. An interesting feature of the church is its leper's squint – a window from which lepers could take part in services without coming into contact with the congregation.

Above: SMA' GLEN, THE ROMAN ENCAMPMENT 1899 44395

The Roman fort at Fendoch was situated at the head of Glen Almond, opposite the mouth of the Sma' Glen in Tayside. It was one of a series of forts known as the Glen Forts, which were constructed at the mouths of glens leading into the Caledonian highlands in AD85. It seems that the Romans intended to use the forts to support an expansion into the area, but those plans were halted by the withdrawal of some forces from Britain for service in the Emperor Domitian's war in Dacia (modern-day Romania). Excavations have shown that the fort at Fendoch was only occupied for a short period. The camp appears to have been deliberately dismantled and its timbers burnt; by AD90 all the forts north of the Forth/Clyde were decommissioned.

FINGAL'S CAVE   *Staffa, Strathclyde*

Lying to the north-east of Iona, the uninhabited island of Staffa is celebrated for its caves and rock formations. Legend has it that the cave was formed when the giant Fingal, or Finn McCool, made the island. Finn is also said to have built the Giant's Causeway in Northern Ireland. Sir Walter Scott visited the phenomenon and said that it was 'one of the most extraordinary places I ever beheld. It exceeded, in my mind, every description I had heard of it … composed entirely of basaltic pillars as high as the roof of a cathedral, and running deep into the rock, eternally swept by a deep and swelling sea, and paved, as it were, with ruddy marble, it baffles all description'.

> *We were put out into boats and lifted by the hissing sea up the pillar stumps to the celebrated Fingal's Cave. A greener roar of waves surely never rushed into a stranger cavern – its many pillars making it look like the inside of an immense organ, black and resounding, and absolutely without purpose, and quite alone, the wide grey sea within and without.*
>
> FELIX MENDELSSOHN 1829

226

The island of Iona, near Mull off the west coast of Scotland, is known as the cradle of Scottish Christianity, or 'The Mecca of Gael'. St Columba built his monastery here in AD563, and it remained his headquarters for 34 years. From here, St Columba converted a large part of Scotland to Christianity.

A Victorian guidebook described the spectacular atmosphere of the ruins: 'They are very different from those of most of the abbeys of England: instead of nestling in some sheltered dale, they stand on the wind-smitten shore of the bare and rocky isle; no groves of trees cluster around their grey walls, half-hiding them from the passer-by, nor does mantling ivy mask the rents which time and man have made. At Iona, the storm howls among its crumbling walls; its massive tower stands four square to all the winds that blow.'

IONA, THE ABBEY,
THE WEST FRONT 1903 50891

THE CATHEDRAL

Iona, Strathclyde

'Iona of my heart, Iona of my love,
Instead of monks' voices there shall be lowing of cattle:
But before the world comes to an end
Iona shall be as it was.'

So said St Columba shortly before he died, according to St Adamnan in his 'Life of St Columba'. Indeed, although monks endured here from the 6th to the 16th centuries (the Benedictines founded a monastery here in 1203), after the Reformation their voices were silent for a long time, and the abbey fell into ruin.

At last, at the beginning of the 20th century, the Duke of Argyll gave the abbey church to the Iona Cathedral Trust in the hope that restoration work might be undertaken; the building was eventually re-roofed, and used for worship again in 1910. In 1938, George Macleod founded the Iona Community and began the restoration of the buildings. Today, modern pilgrims come in their thousands, and the Community lives, worships and teaches here, just as Columba's community and the Benedictine monks did in the past. Photograph 50889 shows the ruins as they were before restoration began – these are the ruins of the Benedictine monastery; little remains today of Columba's community. Nearer the camera is St Oran's Chapel.

St Oran's Chapel (50892, above) dates from the 11th century; in the graveyard beside it, the oldest burial ground in Scotland, are the graves of 48 Scottish kings and chieftains, and the graves of kings of Ireland, France and Norway. One of the kings buried on Iona was Duncan, the king slain in 1040 by Macbeth.

Photograph 50893, opposite, shows the final resting-place of many of the Clan MacLean, looking rather neglected at the time the photograph was taken.

St Martin's cross (50895, right) is the best and most famous of the free-standing tall Celtic crosses that survive on Iona. It dates from the 8th century. It is 17ft high, and carved with biblical scenes on one side, and on the other the 'boss and serpent' design associated with pre-Christian worship.

Above: IONA, ST ORAN'S CHAPEL 1903   50892

Opposite above: IONA, THE ABBEY 1903   50889

Opposite below: IONA, THE TOMBS OF THE MACLEANS 1903   50893

Right: IONA, ST MARTIN'S CROSS 1903   50895

The origins of Celtic Christianity

Celtic culture existed most strongly in Cornwall, Wales, Scotland and Ireland; today it can be traced through language, custom, religion and monuments, especially the Celtic crosses. How did this separate identity come about? From AD313, when the Roman Emperor Constantine legalised Christianity, Celtic Christianity could command followers without fear of prosecution. Constantine's acceptance of Christianity came about when, on the eve of an important battle in northern Italy, he had a dream in which he saw the Chi-Rho sign (the first two letters of Christ's name in Greek), and was told: 'In this sign conquer'; he therefore changed the Roman Labarum, a banner with a wreath-like circle, to include the Chi-Rho sign. He won the battle, and thereafter Christianity was permitted throughout the Roman Empire. It is interesting that Constantine did not become converted himself until he was on his deathbed in AD330 – he clearly wished to hedge his bets!

It is this Chi-Rho sign and the crucifixion that has dominated Celtic crosses. It was not always so, since early Christianity often used the symbol of the fish or the peacock, but this is the origin of the design that appears on many stone crosses today. The purpose of such crosses is not always immediately obvious. Most probably many were markers pointing the way for travellers to a particular religious site, the home of a reclusive hermit or a secret meeting-place for worship. Some were commemorative in recognition of a saint or early king. Others still present a puzzle to historians.

DUNOLLIE CASTLE — *Oban, Strathclyde*

Dunollie Castle stands just to the north of Oban on the west coast of Scotland. Here lived the MacDougalls, the Lords of Lorne, who once owned a third of Scotland; since the 7th century their stronghold has stood on this lofty promontory overlooking the sea. However, the castle we see today dates mainly from the 15th century. Near the castle can be found the Clach a' Choin (the Dog Stone). Legend has it that the giant Fingal tied his dog, Bran, to this stone. Fingal is a figure from early Celtic mythology, a mighty giant, probably the equivalent of the Irish warrior god Fionn MacCumhail (Finn McCool), the greatest of the Celtic heroes.

Top: OBAN, DUNOLLIE CASTLE AND THE DOGSTONE 1901 47513

Above: OBAN, DUNOLLIE CASTLE 1880 O4005

THE GIANT'S CAUSEWAY, THE LOOM 1897 40438

'When the world was moulded and fashioned out of formless chaos, this must have been the bit over – a remnant of chaos'.
So said William Makepeace Thackeray. The Giant's Causeway is in reality a freak of geological nature, which was created by volcanic eruptions and cooling lava, resulting in a compacted mass of around 40,000 mainly hexagonal basalt columns. The effect is of a series of stepping stones, which lead down from the cliffs into the sea. Before the geological origins were understood, this natural wonder was explained in terms of legend: one story says that the Causeway was made by the giant Finn McCool, when he fell in love with a lady giant on the Hebridean island of Staffa, and built the causeway to bring her to Ulster; another interpretation is given on page 232. At the Wishing Arch (40421, overleaf) we see the black basalt overlying the chalk rocks. Its formations look so artificial that over the years various features here have been given fanciful names.

231

Above: THE GIANT'S CAUSEWAY, THE GIANT'S WELL C1897   40425

Right: THE GIANT'S CAUSEWAY, THE WISHING ARCH C1897   40421

Finn McCool's legendary challenge

Finn McCool (Fionn macCumhail) was a legendary figure, the leader of the Fianna, the military elite of ancient Ireland responsible for guarding the High King; the Fianna are said to have been founded in the 4th century BC by the High King Fiachadh. Finn organised the Fianna as defenders of the rights of the Irish people and as models of chivalry and justice. According to one legend, Finn made the Giant's Causeway (in fact volcanic rock formations) on the coast of Ireland. He grew angry when a Scottish giant questioned his strength, and threw a rock across the Irish Sea to Scotland as a challenge. The Scottish giant immediately threw a rock back to Finn, saying that he could not take up the challenge because he could not swim across to Ireland; so Finn tore down huge pieces of rock and used them to build a causeway that ran from Ireland to Scotland. The Scottish giant crossed over to Finn's house, but Finn defeated him and chased him back to Scotland, flinging huge lumps of earth after him. One of the large holes he made became Lough Neagh, the largest lake in Ireland; and one of the lumps of earth fell into the Irish Sea, and became the Isle of Man.

THE ARDBOE CROSS

Coagh, Northern Ireland

COAGH, THE ARDBOE CROSS C1950 C585301

This elaborate cross, one of the best preserved Celtic crosses in Northern Ireland, probably dates from the 10th century; it stands near the site of a 6th-century monastery. Almost 20ft tall, it is richly carved with many scenes from the scriptures, including Adam and Eve, Daniel in the den of lions, and Christ's birth, miracles and crucifixion.

INDEX

FREE PRINT OF YOUR CHOICE

Mounted Print
Overall size 14 x 11 inches (355 x 280mm)

CHOOSE A PHOTOGRAPH FROM THIS BOOK

Choose any Frith photograph in this book.

Simply complete the voucher opposite and return it with your remittance for £3.50
(to cover postage and handling) and we will print the photograph of your choice in SEPIA
(size 11 x 8 inches) and supply it in a cream mount with a burgundy rule line
(overall size 14 x 11 inches).

Offer valid for delivery to UK addresses only.

PLUS: **Order additional Mounted Prints at HALF PRICE - £8.50 each** (normally £17.00)
If you would like to order more Frith prints from this book, possibly as gifts for friends and
family, you can buy them at half price (with no additional postage and handling costs).

PLUS: **Have your Mounted Prints framed**
For an extra £14.95 per print you can have your mounted print(s) framed in an elegant
polished wood and gilt moulding, overall size 16 x 13 inches
(no additional postage and handling required).

IMPORTANT!

These special prices are only available if you use this form to order.

You must use the ORIGINAL VOUCHER on this page (no copies permitted).

We can only despatch to one UK address.

This offer cannot be combined with any other offer.

Send completed voucher form to:
The Francis Frith Collection, Frith's Barn, Teffont, Salisbury, Wiltshire SP3 5QP

Voucher for **FREE** and Reduced Price Frith Prints

*Please do not photocopy this voucher. Only the original is valid,
so please fill it in, cut it out and return it to us with your order.*

Picture ref no	Page no	Qty	Mounted @ £8.50	Framed + £17.00	Total Cost £
		1	Free of charge*	£	£
			£8.50	£	£
			£8.50	£	£
			£8.50	£	£
			£8.50	£	£
			£8.50	£	£

Please allow 28 days for delivery. Offer available to one UK address only

* Post & handling		£3.50
Total Order Cost		£

Title of this book . . . .

I enclose a cheque/postal order for £ . . . .
made payable to 'The Francis Frith Collection'

OR please debit my Mastercard / Visa / Maestro card,
details below

Card Number

Issue No (Maestro only)   Valid from (Maestro)

Expires   Signature

Name Mr/Mrs/Ms . . . .
Address . . . .
. . . .
. . . .
. . . . Postcode . . . .
Daytime Tel No . . . .
Email . . . .

ISBN 1-84589-276-3   Valid to 31/12/09

Free Print – see overleaf

Can you help us with information about any of the Frith photographs in this book?

We are gradually compiling an historical record for each of the photographs in the Frith archive. It is always fascinating to find out the names of the people shown in the pictures, as well as insights into the shops, buildings and other features depicted.

If you recognize anyone in the photographs in this book, or if you have information not already included in the author's caption, visit the Frith website at www.francisfrith.com and add your memories.

Our production team

Frith books are produced by a small dedicated team at offices in the converted Grade II listed 18th-century barn at Teffont near Salisbury, illustrated above. Most have worked with The Francis Frith Collection for many years. All have in common one quality: they have a passion for The Francis Frith Collection. The team is constantly expanding, but currently includes:

Paul Baron, Jason Buck, John Buck, Jenny Coles, Heather Crisp, David Davies, Natalie Davis, Louis du Mont, Isobel Hall, Chris Hardwick, Neil Harvey, Julian Hight, Peter Horne, James Kinnear, Karen Kinnear, Tina Leary, Stuart Login, Sue Molloy, Sarah Roberts, Kate Rotondetto, Eliza Sackett, Terence Sackett, Sandra Sampson, Adrian Sanders, Sandra Sanger, Julia Skinner, Lewis Taylor, Will Tunnicliffe, David Turner and Ricky Williams.